UNDER BOW BELLS

Books by Joseph McCulloch

A Parson in Revolt
The Divine Drama
The Faith that must Offend
We have our Orders
The Trumpet Shall Sound
Medway Adventure
The Door of the Cave
Between God and Man – the Essential Bible

UNDER BOW BELLS

Dialogues with Joseph McCulloch

SHELDON PRESS
LONDON

First published in Great Britain in 1974 by
Sheldon Press
Marylebone Road, London NW1 4DU

Printed in Great Britain by
William Clowes & Sons, Limited
London, Beccles and Colchester

ISBN 0 85969 028 8

To the Worshipful Company of Grocers
since 1456
joint-patrons with the Archbishop of Canterbury
of the Church of St Mary-le-Bow
in the City of London

Contents

Acknowledgements

Joseph McCulloch and the publishers wish to acknowledge their gratitude to: Professor Sir Alfred Ayer; the Rt Hon. James Callaghan M.P.; Lord David Cecil; Lord Clark; Margaret Drabble; Joyce Grenfell; Sheila Hancock; Jacquetta Hawkes; James Laver; Bernard Levin; Michael McCrum; Yehudi Menuhin; Jonathan Miller; Malcolm Muggeridge; Edna O'Brien; Lord Olivier; Diana Rigg; Tom Stoppard; Katharine Whitehorn; and the Rt Hon. Shirley Williams M.P. for permission to use their respective dialogues. Also to Lucinda Gane for transcribing the dialogues from the tape-recordings, and to Betty McCulloch for editing and preparing the transcripts for publication.

Introduction

> I wonder that you will still be talking, Signior Benedick; nobody marks you.
>
> SHAKESPEARE *Much Ado About Nothing*

> When you fall into a man's conversation, the first thing you should consider is, whether he has a greater inclination to hear you, or that you should hear him.
>
> STEELE *The Spectator* No. 49

Some people are born communicators. Some, no doubt, achieve the ability to communicate, and others have communicating thrust upon them. But certain people seem naturally endowed with the faculty of imparting what they think and feel to others by a knack of sharing themselves with others. In any walk of life and in any age this gift has always conferred a considerable personal advantage, but in our own age and in an increasing number of avocations it has become practically the most valued of all talents. The paradox is that though today the means of communication have increased vastly in scope and influence, the number of effective communicators is still comparatively small. Many are called to communicate, but few are chosen.

There is evidently far more to the art of communication than the ability to talk, however fluently and ably. The best talkers may have a great deal to say, but yet communicate very little. All depends in this art on a certain vibration of identity between the talker and his audience. The mass media have multiplied talkers delivering quantities of information to multitudes who hear but do not really mark them. The miracle of communication happens only when between the talker and the listener or between the writer and the reader there is a recognition that they have something in common with one another behind, beyond and within the flux of words. The logic of their difference as individuals remains, but it is subordinated for the time being to a consciousness of community. The reader or the listener feels that somehow he knows the writer or the speaker in a personal relationship.

Hence the emergence of popular communicators who wield

in our society a powerful influence in forming public opinion and determining the contemporary mood, simply because large numbers of people feel the vibration of personal identity with them. They are the common man, only more articulate. For that reason, whoever seeks to know and understand what the common man of today thinks and feels would do well to listen to and learn from members of this select and motley band who, when they talk or write, are always widely heeded. In communicating with the communicators one not only discovers what and how to communicate, but also comes to believe, with John MacMurray, that there is a common philosophy embodied in the modern world, if only we could find it and express it.

THE EXCOMMUNICATED CHURCH

The foregoing now seems self-evident. But I myself realized it only by slow and painful stages. That was no doubt because I went straight from Oxford into the ranks of an institution which, for all its liberal comprehensiveness, is nevertheless locked within its own system of thought, structures and traditions, and for that reason goes on talking, with comparatively few marking it. When I became an Anglican parson in 1931, the strange duplicate process was already far advanced whereby while the world was de-spiritualizing itself, the Church had allowed itself to become increasingly disincarnated. If its members might profess to be not of this world, they were certainly not really in it, despite the original dominical instruction that they should somehow be both.

The disincarnation was manifest in the tacit assumption that Churchmanship was of this world a thing apart. What was especially disconcerting to the eager spirits of many young men who went into the ordained ministry of the Church was the confining process which within a few years stereotyped them into parochial clergymen, a curiously rarified profession in the twentieth century world. Most perforce succumbed to the process, and were duly imprisoned in the mould which the isolation of the Church in the world imposed. But with many the uneasy feeling persisted that they had become rather like the Lowells of Boston who, when they were not talking to the Cabots, talked only to God. In an age of managers, financiers, technicians and accountants, what they had to say sounded even in their own ears curiously beside the point. So they talked mostly to each other, or to the dwindling, predominantly female faithful. One caustic observer commented that the job of the average clergyman was to be warden of a hen roost.

Perhaps the chief irony of the situation lay in the fact that, whereas once the clergy wielded powerfully a threat of excommunication over the world, now the world had virtually excommunicated them. They could not help being aware, more or less painfully, that they were regarded as having chosen not a cure but a sinecure, and were amiably disregarded in it. Sometimes they tried talking to the world at large, usually raising their voices as though addressing the deaf, but their evangelistic zeal, unless boosted with all the expensive techniques of commercial advertising, made little impression, and was treated by most people either with mild amusement or with distaste. Even when the clergy spoke quietly and reasonably, the world had so long ceased to mark them that what they were trying to say was usually misunderstood or misinterpreted. Dialogue between the Church and the world was, with rare exceptions, as good as dead.

THE CHIEF IMPEDIMENT

This was the unsatisfactory predicament in which, with sundry other young men, I found myself in the thirties. I had become an officer of an institution which, as I believed, had more important things to say to the world than any other, but found that the chief impediment to getting them said effectively was the nature and situation of the institution itself. I could not number myself among those who decided that it was futile to go on beating one's wings against the bars of ecclesiastical confinement, that it was best to emulate the Vicar of Bray and accommodate to the Church's prevailing mood, and that the cloth was cut, and the pattern predetermined; what could not be cured must be endured.

I persisted in the conviction that it was disloyal to one's original vocation to acquiesce in so ignominious a role. Hence for upwards of ten years I went restlessly about from parish to parish, seeking a radically new pattern of churchmanship. I achieved no more in my attempt to move the monolith establishment than a gadfly on the back of a mammoth. A series of books in which I sought to express what I saw hampering the Church in its essential task and to press for certain radical reforms, gained more attention and agreement from non-members than from members of the Church. In the last of these books I argued that it was the so-called establishment of the Church which put it on the wrong foot vis-à-vis the contemporary world, and that a new possibility of communication would be opened up, if this status were voluntarily renounced, at whatever cost. William Temple, who had just gone to be Archbishop of Canterbury, was much in favour of my publishing this book, which he had read in typescript, though he himself did not think that the time was ripe for disestablishment. He talked to me freely about his own hopes to make the Church more effective in the modern world, and took trouble to teach me how one can work within the limitations of an imperfect institution and yet be free to go on seeking its radical reform, provided one was willing to stay uninvolved in its power structures. Soon after his untimely death, I came across this passage in Jeremy Taylor: 'It were better that a man imagine what his religion is than what his church is, for a religion that is true today will be so for ever, but a church may betray her trust.' I saw in these words the gist of what Temple had taught me, and the corroboration of what under his influence kept me within the Church but somewhat paradoxically set me free of it.

THE MASS MEDIA

By the thirties a quite new medium of communication had become part of daily life, and was rapidly extending its *imperium* over the whole social field. Nothing so much exposed the Church's predicament as the arrival of radio broadcasting. It fell to my lot over the next twenty years to gain a good deal of experience of the new medium, both in radio and television, chiefly under the aegis of the B.B.C. department of religious broadcasting.

From its inception this particular department was hamstrung by the Church itself, which required as a priority that the various denominations should be given an equitable share of broadcasting time. This meant in effect that those who directed the department—very much a pioneering task—were hampered in their chief priority of finding and training gifted communicators within the Church as a whole who could gain a fresh hearing for the Christian point of view. Instead, the general impact of religious broadcasting was to reflect all too accurately the inability of the Church to understand the given world, and so to corroborate the widespread conception of its religion as an irrelevant anachronism. That is not to say that there were not some among the many religious broadcasters (mostly clergymen) who showed a degree of mastery of the new mass medium, but, with rare exceptions, they were not used often enough to establish themselves as widely-known communicators, and could do little to change the fixed idea that Churchmen were more suited to pulpiteering than broadcasting. That was always the millstone about our necks, though at the time it was difficult to see why an institution which had so many men accustomed to public speaking should be at such a disadvantage when the audience was unseen.

Soon after I began to be employed in broadcasting, I started to write regularly for mass-circulation periodicals, and found that the same basic difficulties had to be surmounted in this medium as in the other. It was not merely a matter of mastering techniques, for example, of learning to talk conversationally rather than oratorically, or to write informally rather than pedantically. In fact, these techniques could not be mastered successfully until one had first gained an imaginative understanding of the listeners or readers, so that one no longer talked or wrote *to* them but rather, as it were *with* them. What was required was the art, not of monologue, but of dialogue, of knowing what was probably in the other person's mind, and meeting it more than halfway. But that itself presupposed that one was habitually very much in the world. For the parson living in his rarified atmosphere it was especially difficult to become the common man, only more articulate.

THE WAY BACK INTO THE WORLD

The war brought many, myself among them, to a point of departure. I spent the first few years of it as a chaplain (C of E) in the armed forces, and found in much discussion of the Church with the rank and file (most of whom professed little or no religion, except titularly), a surprising degree of interest in the subject, and of sympathy with my cause of achieving a Church with greater freedom and elasticity of mind.

In mid-war I returned to parochial life, and looked for a parish where it could safely be said that the Church was not merely moribund but virtually beyond resuscitation. In such a place a new pattern of communication between Church and world might be achievable, unfettered by the demands of existing forms and structures. One might in fact be really free of the Church and more in touch with the world. The parish church at Chatham seemed at the time to have arrived, most opportunely for me, *in extremis*, and I was duly presented to the living. So, for the rest of the forties, I was allowed to make the fullest use by the Medway of the *carte blanche* thus given me.

I decided at the outset to go back to first principles, to the essentials of the pattern of human group-life which had originated the Christian movement in history. This primarily was what the Church had to communicate in the world. The main thing was to get on talking rather than bowing terms again with those who, though they did not say 'Lord, Lord', were by no means the enemies of Christ. The war itself made the circumstances unusually favourable: there were many who saw the war not merely as a disaster but also as a creative opportunity to seek the remedy for the ills of civilization and who felt that much strenuous thinking had to be done about the deeper issues and problems which the war had exposed. It was possible in such a situation to get people thinking constructively together about the question behind all the questions, that concerning the nature and destiny of mankind.

The first requisite was to find a meeting-point for a heterogeneous group who might realize a degree of community at that level of common concern. I had at my disposal a church-building and my own home, which was not a parsonage but merely one of a row of terraced houses. The church-building was unusable for my purpose; in any case, apart from its design as a place where a thousand people could hear a pulpit monologue, it had long been deserted by all but an exiguous handful in the neighbourhood. My own home and family therefore became the natural focus of a group, young, middle-aged and old, who found a common interest in meeting frequently in my house to share their ideas and views. Even when the group grew too numerous to accommodate and had to find larger meeting-places in the town, my house still remained its principal focus.

My own function was difficult to define: it was simply to be there, and learn the knack of directing without leading, to avoid any attempt to persuade or force the pace, and to show no desire to indoctrinate or proselytize. Among the chief hindrances to the Church in its task of communicating is the parsonic *persona*, which is that of one who will still be talking though nobody marks him, because he regards it as his divine vocation to do so. He claims, as an officer of a Church commissioned to go out into the world and make disciples of all nations, that in talking he is fulfilling his orders. Whereas what I began to learn in the Medway group was that in listening and questioning in an atmosphere of free and open discussion he might get much more effectively to the necessary *point d'appui*. I made no attempt to bring in the subject of religion at any point, except when asked as one who ought to know something about it. In the course of my years by the Medway it is noteworthy that the church-building became considerably and regularly frequented for worship, especially by the young.

QUESTIONS ARISING

In a book which I wrote after a few years of this experiment*, I described its creative impact on the immediate neighbourhood, and the thinking which had emerged as its substantial philosophy. Behind the issues of politics, industry and social life, we had come to see how little we really understood of man and his nature, especially in the field of his varied relationships with others. As a working hypothesis, we agreed that the main relationships were

* *Medway Adventure*. Michael Joseph 1942.

those between the generations, between male and female, and between worker and fellow-worker, and we sought the essential principles whereby a pattern of true community could be achieved in them. I am not concerned here to elaborate on the context of so much thought and discussion, except to say that one of its effects was to make members of the group active and articulate in local councils, education and industry, and a new impetus and social concern were discernible throughout the neighbourhood. My immediate point is that some mensurable progress had been made to remedy the dissociation of the Church and the world, between liturgy and life. The process of ecclesiastical disincarnation was in fact capable of being arrested, and the Church could be envisaged as very much in the world. This had been made possible by seeking a new beginning in the actual world, no longer centred and contained in the church-building; most of all, by creating a situation in which the role of the parson was not that of a sectarian indoctrinator and recruiting officer, but of one who sought with all kinds of others the answers to the questions which are raised at depth in this bewildered age.

When I went from the Medway Towns I was convinced, whether or not the official Church pursued its way regardless (as indeed it did), that the future of the Christian institutions would be determined by their ability, or otherwise, to resume essential creative dialogue with the world at large. That would obviously depend on how quickly they could change and liberate themselves in a rapidly changing society. The odds looked very much against it. But my piece of field-work by the Medway had gone as far as I could take it, and there were still certain questions to which I was seeking my own answers, and must seek them elsewhere; especially, how the liturgy could again communicate new life within the Church itself, and by what means the Church's scriptures could be presented so that far more people could read them.

I was again fortunate in being given a place where I could work out my answers to these questions: the charge of a midland parish with a majestically superb church-building. In brief, during the decade of the fifties which I spent in that parish, the answers which worked out in practice were, first, that the existing liturgy becomes astonishingly, communicatively alive if the celebrant serves merely as the integrating person in a ritual act in which the rest of the laity have regular active parts to play; and, secondly, that the Bible in the authorized version can be made fascinatingly readable if three-quarters of its inessential material is omitted, and the rest arranged and presented in modern typography to show the unity and continuity of its theme. My own attempt at producing this essential Bible was published at the close of that decade.* If I were ever to revise it, I would reduce the material still further, to a book of no more than 150,000 words.

THE POST-WAR CHURCH

Towards the close of the fifties C. G. Jung wrote in his *Dreams, Memories and Reflections*:

> We have plunged down a cataract of progress which sweeps us on into the future with ever wilder violence the farther it takes us from our roots. Once the past has been breached . . . there is no stopping the forward motion. But it is precisely the loss of our connection with the past, our uprootedness, which has given rise to the 'discontents' of civilization. . . . We rush impetuously into novelty, driven by a mounting sense of insufficiency, dissatisfaction and restlessness.

This describes fairly accurately (though I would question his use of the word 'progress') the post-war course of events. What is especially remarkable is the increasing momentum of the changes in our society. Those who survive in the seventies are conscious of a feverish outpouring of ideas, 'news', events, which can be fitted into no general context or scheme of continuity, except perhaps that of an accelerating whirligig. The optimists see us living in a creative melting-pot; the pessimists refer frequently to the precipitous cliff and the Gadarene swine.

The plight of the Church since the war has become increasingly accentuated, precisely because the past which has been breached belongs very considerably to its own history. The roots of the civilization which is suffering even wilder violence of change, are in the Christian religion. If the Church is to communicate with such a world, of what must it dispossess itself? Herbert Butterfield ends his *Christianity and History* with the words: 'We can never face the future with sufficient elasticity of mind especially if we are locked in the contemporary system of thought. . . . We can do worse than remember a principle: Hold to Christ and for the rest be totally uncommitted.' This is sound advice, but extremely difficult for institutions dominated by the tyranny of their own past to put into practice. The roots of the Church are in Christ, and must remain so, however rootless the contemporary world. The Church has its age-old liturgy and its canonical scriptures, which in a predominantly atheistic world have little relevance or use. But these it cannot abandon. They carry through the ages the essential truths

* *Between God and Man*. Hutchinson 1960.

it has to communicate. In such a situation, perhaps it is enough merely to hang on and wait for a return to the roots, to the old religion.

The alternative which inevitably appealed to some within the Church was to bring it up-to-date, to present a 'with-it' Church by various attempts to incorporate into its activities 'stunts' and novelties which were thought to correspond with the changing mood of the age, and so give religion a new look. Regrettably, these failed to arrest the decline in the number of the Church's adherents, and made little or no contribution to the solution of the basic problem, which is how to communicate the essential religion of Christ. The postwar world might well be described in the words addressed to a former generation: 'We have piped unto you, and ye have not danced; we have mourned unto you and ye have not wept.' The 'with-it' clergyman had not changed his *persona*; it merely rattled!

A far more searching dilemma of integrity was felt especially by the more considering parson. For some time science had wielded an authority which had once been given to the doctrines of the Church. But in the fifties the wind of change began to veer away from science in a renewed search for the answers to the existential questions. When sometimes these questions were brought to the parson, he was tempted to answer them as though his field of knowledge was similar to that of the various departmentalized branches of scientific learning. Indeed, the official Church went in for Christian Inquiry Centres, which dealt out this type of stock answer, and for a while did a brisk business. But the distance between unfaith and faith in the modern world is far more, a whole dimension more, than a matter of crossing the frontier between ignorance of orthodox Christian doctrine and knowledge of it. What the Church has to communicate cannot be communicated in that way. Faith is a gift which can be caught, but not taught. The parson is rather a poet than a grammarian. He is concerned primarily with the truth and beauty of the poem, not with its technique or its syntax, or even with its structure and imagery. With the modern inquirer, he has to find a meeting-place far further back, where the universe and life itself are accepted beyond any analysing of their constituents. And there he perceives that the inquirer is not really asking, 'How can religion solve my problems?' whether of philosophy, psychology or morals, but, granted these problems can or cannot be solved, 'Where do I belong, and what is it all about anyhow?'. Hence the parson, if he is to keep his integrity, must refuse to superimpose Christianity upon the atheistic mind. Since the real struggle of the modern world in which he must be engaged is that between atheism and Christ, what he has to communicate, in the midst of all the ambiguities of the Christian religion, is no religious expertise but the understanding of faith and the special grace of relationship in the community of man with his neighbour, which is realized through faith in Christ.

THE CHURCH AND TELEVISION

The fifties of this century were particularly remarkable as the decade in which television became the dominant mass medium of communication. Its most notable general effect was an acceleration of the restless mood of the age, especially among the rising generation, who in fact became moulded more by what they saw and heard on television than by any other influence. Although religion had its share of this new mass medium, little change was effected in the situation of the Church vis-à-vis contemporary society. The chief difficulty lay in the nature of television broadcasting itself, in which each department had to justify its existence by the success or failure of its power to attract and hold the maximum number of viewers. What was therefore demanded was 'lively' viewing material. A discussion on any subject was not 'good television' unless it was animated, even acrimonious, controversy. The sight of two people talking reasonably together in a real dialogue, where each sought by exchange of views to seek a common mind, was not thought likely to hold the millions, and was therefore allowed only when most of the millions were not likely to be viewing. Impassioned argument or a collection of monologuers airing bewilderingly conflicting opinions, with a professional anchorman, a referee keeping the ring, made the usual pattern of allegedly discussion programmes. Religious television, perforce following this pattern, more often than not succeeded in generating more heat than light, and the Christian case seldom emerged with any clarity of expression. It was sometimes magnificent as entertainment, but was not the real war, as far as communicating what truth the Church has to share with the world is concerned. The inevitable tendency has been to make religious programmes practically indistinguishable from other discussion programmes on current affairs.

Ironically, it is probable that broadcasting as a new profession has drawn off quite a number of those who in former times might have gone into the orders of the Church, and thereby added to the difficulty of recruiting men of good brain and grain into the Christian ministry at a time when they are especially needed. It is not unlikely that several of those who have become eminent as television 'wheel-horses' might by now have adorned the bench of bishops! On the whole, television has increased rather than lessened the inability of the Church to influence an age which restlessly seeks to draw out of its treasure constantly new things, and flings away the old. The medium itself is largely in the hands of those who are predominantly creatures of the age, and therefore not greatly interested in the necessary relation between roots and fruits.

MEETING ON THE SAME PREMISES

It is told of Sydney Smith that he and another canon of St Paul's were walking through an alley-way, from either side of which two women were standing on their doorsteps, hurling abuse at each other. 'You see,' said Smith, 'why those women can never agree. They are arguing from totally different premises.' It seemed to me at the close of the fifties that before all else what had to be achieved was a common ground between the Church and the world. It was little use to go on talking from different premises. At that time it so happened that the Church of St Mary-le-Bow, nominally famous because of Bow Bells, stood a derelict ruin in Cheapside, having been almost totally devastated by bombing in 1941. The reigning Archbishop suggested that I might like to go there, and seeing this as virtually the offer of yet another *carte blanche*, I accepted. While the very considerable sum of money needed for the rebuilding was being raised (it was the most costly of all the Wren churches), I had four years in which to draw the threads together, and make some coherent pattern in my own mind of what I had for so many years been seeking.

On the positive side, I had never been anything but convinced that the essential Christian faith was more worth communicating today than any other view of mankind. But what Emil Brünner called the misunderstanding of the Church, a deliberately two-edged phrase, was an increasingly formidable obstacle to its effective communication. The world at large undoubtedly had a mistaken conception of the Church. But no less the Church betrayed a misunderstanding of that world. This duplicate failure was simply because they knew each other no more than superficially; a conversation between them, when it occurred, was, more often than not, inevitably at cross-purposes. The responsibility for that situation the Church had to accept as its own, and take the initiative in remedying it. Since, as William Temple pointed out, the Church is a society which exists primarily for the benefit of non-members, it was clearly at fault in becoming largely preoccupied with its own affairs. On what terms, therefore, would non-Churchmen be interested to accept an invitation to visit church premises simply to talk with Churchmen about the deeper issues which underlie the human situation? Why not the terms of straightforward hospitality? To test this line of reasoning, we restored first the ancient Norman crypt and equipped it with a refectory, and, under the useful title of Christian Agnostics, invited eminent politicians, doctors, writers, theologians, and other professional thinkers to talk together before and after a light supper. Each of these gatherings was limited to twenty people, and proved, certainly from my point of view, a valuable experiment, which influenced my plan for the rebuilding of the main church.

One interesting aspect of these gatherings was that, if there were two theologians present, they tended to inhibit freedom of discussion by talking to each other. I realized from that experience that the Church's role today was far more to learn to listen than to go on talking, especially when it is acting as host to a number of non-Church guests. The only record we have of Jesus of Nazareth *in statu pupillarii* tells of his sitting among the accredited communicators of the day, 'both hearing them, and asking them questions'. That seems to me the part which the contemporary Church has to accept for the time being. When we fall into a man's conversation, it is more important at present we consider that we should hear him. It is undoubtedly a severe discipline, especially when our preconceived idea is that our calling requires us to be constantly bearing witness to the truth of the gospel of Christ. But there are far more ways than one of doing that. The great Christian communicator, Paul, sought to be all things to all men. To achieve that elasticity of mind, the prerequisite is to hear what they have to say, and to be content to do no more than ask them questions. This is especially true in a world in which there is no common philosophy, where all assumptions are questioned and principles are usually identified as prejudices.

A PLACE OF EFFECTIVE COMMUNICATION

It had been painfully obvious for at least thirty years that while the delivery of sermons and addresses could still be valuable as a method of instructing Church adherents (though preaching to the converted usually tends to accentuate the disincarnation of the Church), outside ecclesiastical preserves it was so much water on the duck's back. In the 'no Churchman's land' which stretches between orthodox belief and total disbelief, there is little disposition to listen to religious exhortation and apologetics, which seem so much professional jargon, and are readily suspected of cant, or of being as one wit described it, 'clerical-grey flannel'. Even if we had a Chrysostom preaching away in every pulpit and religious broadcast, the hiatus between the Church and the others would, it anything, become more marked. Jung is right when he says modern man feels that the Church speaks from outside him. There is good reason to think that zealous 'evangelists' do more to heighten resistance to the Church's religion than otherwise. Church-buildings have long been designed to perpetuate this monological method, with rows of pews dominated by the occupant of the pulpit. It is not remarkable that in this age they attract dwindling congregations.

In designing the interior of St Mary-le-Bow, it was manifestly necessary to provide a pattern more adaptable to its actual situation in a non-residential weekday working neighbourhood, one which would be attractive not only to worshippers but also to those, the vast majority, who ordinarily have no use for church-buildings. Otherwise, it might well prove little more than an expensive white elephant in the middle of the already over-churched City of London. I came to the idea of designing it as a centre of dialogue after an experiment in Westminster Abbey. I had been invited by Edward Carpenter to give a series of Advent lunch-hour talks there, and, in view of my distrust of the value of such monologues, we agreed to try instead a series of dialogues together. This experiment, technically difficult to put on in the nave of the Abbey, nevertheless encouraged me in my view that dialogue between two people, which was the earliest form of dramatic art, would prove far more effective and attractive than our existing outworn method of communication. It seemed to me that, at the very least, if there were two speakers visibly on equal terms, people of an enquiring mind might want to listen to their conversation, and judge for themselves in which direction greater truth might be sought. Accordingly, the rebuilt church was provided with two identical pulpits, in which two people might discuss anything under the sun, with difference admittedly, but without inequality. We also provided movable chairs instead of fixed pews, so that an audience might be grouped around the pulpits informally, or even stand about, and come and go, as they pleased. The aim was to achieve a design of an interior which would permit of flexibility, free enquiry and an open mind; a place in fact, of effective communication.

RESUMING THE DIALOGUE WITH THE WORLD

Since the reconstruction of the restored building in June 1964, a weekly dialogue in the Tuesday lunch-break has been a regular event which soon ceased to be experimental and became an accepted and popular feature of the City's working week. Bow Church, as the City calls it, has been for nine centuries at the hub of as lively a concentration of thinking, feeling, questioning, doubting and partly believing people as the world has seen. It is not, therefore, surprising that from the outset the dialogues attracted a 'full house', and throughout a decade of Tuesdays the church has seldom been less than crowded and frequently over-crowded. The audience is drawn mainly from the offices and shops around the church, but a number of people come from further afield, including many visitors from overseas. What proportion of this audience are active members of any church is obviously difficult to assess, but I would guess that it comes mostly from 'no Church-man's land'. Although these people come to listen and have no part in the discussion, they are manifestly very much *in* it, and as an audience have an unusually lively and distinctive character.

At first, I invited only eminent Church spokesmen to occupy the other pulpit, but quickly realized that people were not greatly interested to hear Churchmen talking to each other. Inevitably, the conversation between clerics in the pulpits seemed to the audience to be two people speaking from outside their situation. We were communicating with each other, but not with them. What was needed was the renewal of dialogue with the world as it is.

But who are the spokesmen of that world? I was soon led to the obvious answer. They are the people who, for one reason or another, have already gained a hearing, those to whom the general public are listening and from whom come many of the ideas which inform the contemporary mind—writers, broadcasters, stage and screen personalities, scientists, musicians, architects, politicians, captains of industry—in fact the acknowledged 'communicators' in any of the various departments of modern life. Their attitude to religion may well range from professed atheism through all the shades of the free-thinking spectrum to one or other of the denominational forms of orthodox religious belief. In that especially, they represent the actual world with which the Church should be in dialogue, that is, free and personal communication, about the questions urgent upon man today. I therefore decided that, as a general rule, one pulpit should be occupied by a professing believer in Christ and that to the other pulpit I should invite one who was widely known as a 'communicator' or a distinguished member of another profession, whatever his attitude to religion might be. This, in the event, has proved an effective way of keeping open the dialogue between the Church and the world. Some of the most valuable of the dialogues have been those when the visitor's pulpit has been occupied by a professed atheist or a severe critic of institutional Christianity. For my wife and myself one of the most pleasurable and noteworthy results of entertaining the communicators each Tuesday was that many whom we had not previously met became our personal friends. That is no doubt because one of the chief qualities of distinguished commentators is a gift for making friends. This was borne out by the fact that the audience, who as a rule have never seen them in person, show by their warm reception of them that they feel already in a kind of personal relationship with them.

FREEDOM OF SPEECH

The objection that this was an irreligious use of a sacred building has never been made. Admittedly, the dialogues are not specifically 'religious' in form, being simply free and informal conversations before an audience which enters into them with keen and spontaneous appreciation expressed often in laughter, and always with applause. But the fact that they take place in the presence of the Altar and the Blessed Sacrament and under the Rood, which speak eloquently for themselves, makes it clear to any considering man or woman that the Church's commitment to Christ remains constant amid the restless doubts and questioning of the contemporary world. The Church is seen in the dialogue able to move upon its fixed centre to encompass all the manifold activities and questions of modern man. That is in practice what the Church's apostolicity and incarnation must really mean. Almost invariably in the course of a dialogue, whatever its topic, questions of personal faith are raised, though seldom deliberately introduced, and in these its true value lies, both for the audience and often for the dialoguers themselves. It is somehow easier to speak freely on such matters in that setting than in any other. To hear a non-Churchman express not mere opinion but personal belief about human life, and the guiding principles by which he seeks to live in a society whose landmarks are singularly befogged, is much more remarkable than to hear similar sentiments from a parson.

It may be alleged with some truth that the dialogues may leave only the dustiest of answers in the minds of many of the audience, and I have often been asked to lay on the line more firmly the Christian view. But I remain convinced that when the Churchman is acting as host not only to the visiting speaker but also to all in the audience who are still in 'no Church-man's land', his proper part is to listen and question rather than indoctrinate. I do not think that the Church's case is weakened thereby; on the contrary, there is no need to press it. In entering into any man's conversation, the unecclesiastical Churchman is by no means at a disadvantage if he is seen to recognize himself as one who is still seeking a greater understanding of the truth he knows upon his pulses, and by which he struggles to live. If his own prejudices and presuppositions have to be examined and criticized in the light of common experience, he should have no fear that thereby his faith in Christ can suffer real damage.

The more men delve into the intersubjective or personal field of experience, the nearer they may come to faith in the truth of Christ. Effective communication is only possible when it is intersubjective, the meeting of persons who are seeking truth and meaning in existence at whatever level, and who find, whatever their difference of approach or terminology, that what they share is often of far more value and significance than the things which separate them. Frequently, what is communicated thus between the pulpits is itself communicated to the heterogenous assembly of listeners. It is only when I have forgotten the severe discipline of seeking to hear and understand, and revert to the defensive aggressiveness of which the Churchman is too often guilty, that the dialogue fails in its purpose. But while I keep firmly in mind the very obvious fact that I have entered into conversation with an unusually gifted personality, and seek to hear and draw from him or her what he or she has got to impart, I am myself enriched, and as a result many will go from the dialogue with minds more open or self-critical.

Essentially, commitment to Christ is to be obedient to the Spirit, not merely in the Church but more especially in the world. We have to beware lest we mistake commitment to an ecclesiastical fixity of life for an obedience to the dynamic of divine things in our own age. History has abundant evidence to show how tragically that error has in the past prevented the Church from being open to the Word of God in an age of creativity and social change. That is not to say that everything in the confusion of ideas and attitudes which influence people in our time points to an emergent truth; it is to say that only if we learn and understand what they are, we may discern how we can go to meet the future, serving the needs of mankind with more certain knowledge and greater flexibility of mind.

THE OBJECTIVE OF THE DIALOGUE

In making this first selection for publication of twenty dialogues out of more than four hundred in the past decade, the aim has been to show the freedom of approach to a wide range of topics which this use of a church-building allows. Usually, the topic for discussion was not decided upon until the 'communicator' and myself had met for an hour or so immediately before the dialogue. There was, therefore, the minimum of time for preparation. Indeed, once we had chosen the topic and agreed upon the starting point for discussion, we preferred to leave it at that stage, and, especially if we had not previously met personally, used the rest of the time before our occupation of the twin pulpits in getting to know each other and conversing about other things. This ensured the spontaneity and informality of the dialogue, and thereby heightened its interest for the audience.

Sometimes my guest would want to get something in particular said and to make certain points, but, on the whole, genuine communication happened best when the discussion was allowed to move freely, without lines too carefully laid down beforehand; in fact not a tram, but a bus! Because we were genuinely seeking to arrive at the place of common understanding, and my part was chiefly to make that possible by listening and questioning, the dialogue was not an exercise in dialectics, where one speaker advances a proposition to be argued.

An ancient precedent for the use of two pulpits in the church was the medieval disputation between clerics, but this I had rejected for reasons given above, as no longer an effective method in the modern world. I was seeking not to expose fallacies or demonstrate the validity of Church doctrine, but simply to establish a relationship between myself as a Churchman and a guest who had provably created a vibration of identity with many in the world at large, and therefore was an articulate representative of what many thought and felt. For that purpose, two people seeking only to put their own points of view would demonstrate only a failure to communicate, and exemplify the disincarnation of the Church.

Because the City's lunch-break is now mostly limited to three-quarters of an hour, perforce the dialogue had to be kept strictly to thirty-five minutes' length. Writing about the Bow dialogues in a publication entitled *The Secular and The Sacred*, Brian Frost takes up this point, as follows,

> Of course, the time is short for this form of encounter and there is little opportunity for development of a cogent case, nor do the gathered assembly participate other than by intense listening . . . Yet undoubtedly the lives of public men and women have been opened up in a new way and the Church itself has been seen to be willing to approach the world in a humbler role.

From what I have written above, it may be seen that my aim has never been to establish a cogent case, but to learn the first steps in restoring a relationship of understanding between Church and world. Despite the shortness of the dialogues' duration, this aim has proved practicable, as a perusal of the following may show. In the process, an opportunity has been provided for many people to discover that they can actually enjoy an occasion in a church, even while it starts them thinking, perhaps more strenuously than usual. No doubt the effort in many cases is abortive. Even so, the Church has nothing to lose and a great deal to gain by stimulating deeper thought on contemporary issues in the context of its own faith and on its own ground.

LEARNING AND UNLEARNING

One of the clearest lessons learned after so many dialogues is that the differences between Churchmen are often wider than those between faith and unfaith. I found on many an occasion that it was much easier to communicate with those who professed no Christian allegiance than with those who did, especially when the professed faithful seemed to equate Christianity with a particular moralism. I myself draw a distinction between morals and ethics which non-Churchmen are quicker to grant than some fellow-Churchmen. If one believes in God as known in Christ, morals are ethics with the added dimension of a sense of sin, that is, a feeling that in failing to act according to one's highest imagination of ethical imperatives, one offends against that which is ontologically behind, beyond and within the flux of things. Because this age is very much concerned with urgent issues which raise fundamental moral questions, this theme recurred constantly throughout the dialogues. It is in this field of discussion that the misunderstanding of the Church, in both senses, is made particularly apparent. Because dialogue between the world and the Church has for so long been virtually non-existent, the popular concept of what the Church means by a sense of sin is loosely understood as 'guilt complex', though not by any means what Freud would have meant in using that term.

In effect, the world sees the Church more or less as the Pharisees who of old loaded mankind with unnecessary and grievous burdens of conscience. On the other hand, the Church is apt to see the world as wilfully blind to the palpable evidence of man's essential nature as a moral being, that is, a creature endowed with the faculty of determining his destiny by decisions concerning right and wrong, and therefore in a perpetually critical predicament. These are the different premises from which the argument between believer and non-believer is unlikely to reach a real place of meeting. But neither in fact corresponds with the actual situation of the world or the Church. When the miracle of real communication happens, the intelligent non-believer is willing to admit that what the Church really means by a sense of sin does correspond with something in the common experience of men and women. It is the actual word rather than its existential meaning which he rejects, because it connotes ideas which inept religious teaching about sin in the Church's past has left in the popular mind. He has to unlearn many such ideas before he can hear what the Church is actually trying to say. In Christian history Gresham's law has inexorably obtained; much bad thinking has tended to drive out the good. The real religion of Jesus has to be heard again, free from the encrustations of centuries of theologizing about it.

But the Church itself has no less to unlearn certain attitudes and ideas which derive from too sharp a distinction between what are termed the secular and the sacred. The activity of the Spirit can never be confined within the preserves of Christian denominations. The most discernible expression of that activity in the modern world is the converging movement which is bringing into closer relationship not only the Christian denominations but also, and far more significantly, the great historic religions of the world. Needs must, not when the devil drives, but when the Spirit leads towards the essential unity of mankind. The emphasis which Jesus unequivocally laid, not upon verbal professions of orthodoxy but upon the motives and the moral imagination which determine what people are and do, is the real meeting-point of the Church and the world. Hence to judge the present world outside the Church as disregarding the existential moral issues of the human condition is to misunderstand it. Communicating with communicators almost invariably reveals as lively an awareness of those issues as can be found in the Church itself. The atheist and the agnostic (the latter far more representative of the general modern attitude than the former) both recognize an element beyond the physical and psychophysical. Their difference from the professing believer is an inability to accept the Church's identification of that mysterious element as belonging to a spiritual order of being which both transcends and rules the universe. But they no less share with the believer the realization that man in society must acknowledge certain moral imperatives, and it is the characteristic of our age to seek to define anew what those imperatives are. The essays of Iris Murdoch on *The Sovereignty of Good* make this abundantly clear.

POSTSCRIPT

It remains to add an explanatory note about the editing of the twenty dialogues which the publishers have selected and present in this volume. As a literary form, live dialogue cannot be reproduced *verbatim*. When we talk with each other freely and spontaneously, we search for the right words to express the ideas which the interchange with another mind sparks off in our own. Hence we are apt to repeat ourselves or to leave some things half-expressed. To render conversation into a presentable literary style requires a good deal of pruning of unnecessary words and a certain amount of supplying words and phrases which will enable the reader to follow the essential discussion. The audiences who actually see and hear the speakers are carried along by their own involvement in the dialogue. In fact, they supply by this lively participation in it, a kind of extra dimension which facilitates the communication of ideas, in much the same way as in the theatre the audience helps the actors to interpret the theme of the drama. In presenting the dialogue to the reader, therefore, a kind of preliminary distilling process is needed in order that he may be given a coherent and easily intelligible account of what was essentially communicated between the pulpits. At the same time, it is also necessary not to lose in this process the flow and individuality of the conversations. They are not literary exercises after the manner of Plato or W. S. Landor, but records of what two people actually said to each other.

The dialogues were recorded on tape and then faithfully transcribed with meticulous adherence to Carroll's principle: 'Take care of the sense, and the sounds will take care of themselves.' In the following selection, the publishers have chosen only dialogues in which I myself was one of the speakers. For that reason, it seemed best to me not to edit the transcripts myself, lest I was tempted at times to give myself the benefit of the doubt! Luckily, I had close at hand one who often knows better than I what I am trying to say, and is also especially skilful at extracting order out of what to me appears chaos. She also had the advantage of knowing personally the other parties in the conversations. Therefore the task fell to my wife so to edit the transcripts that they substantially reproduce most of the letter and very much of the spirit of the original interchange. She submitted her edited versions to the other speakers for his or her *imprimatur*, and when that was received, I read them with much admiration and recollected pleasure.

They came to me as I read them, with surprisingly new interest. Perhaps that was because they had been chosen almost at random, certainly without any intention of specific grouping or a common theme. Despite that, a number of characteristics or attitudes are discernible as common to all of them in varying degree. Certain themes or questions keep recurring, whatever the actual topic under discussion, presumably because they are very much in the contemporary mind. I think that the reader should be left to discern them for himself. But it is undoubtedly of significance that twenty such distinctive and highly individualized communicators in a bewildered age, when the lack of common faith is thought to bode the impending dissolution of our society, should affirm in their different ways the same imperatives and values as the essential stuff of human life. Perhaps we are nearer to the discovery and expression of a common faith and philosophy than the cynics and the pessimists opine. It would be interesting to discover whether twenty more of the dialogues selected at random would further substantiate this hope. For my part, I have gained from this decade of dialogues a consistent impression that, despite all the adverse signs of our times, there is a counterbalancing force of mind and spirit which is on the side of growth in our humanity.

But there is no mistaking the general attitude towards the Church as it is. The most intelligent and gifted among us, while they are far from antagonistic, see the Church as still lagging far behind or failing to be on terms with the widening of consciousness which is shaping the future of mankind. How far that view is justified is for us in the Church to assess with self-critical and open minds. One thing is plain—it cannot be ignored, and we must seek the remedy. In seeking it, I am convinced from experience that the admonition of St Paul is of immediate and practical importance. 'Be not forgetful to entertain strangers, for thereby some have entertained angels unawares.'

What I myself have learned from this decade of dialogues could no doubt fill many pages. Of one thing I am quite certain: the misunderstanding of the Church could be removed and its greater incarnation in the world achieved, if its buildings were adapted for free and open communication with the many who, for one reason and another, are now strangers to them. Most people today are uncommitted to any form of religious faith. But many feel the need to put down roots in a bewildering, unstable age, and might find their need answered if the Church were heard to speak again with authority and not as the scribes.

I have had the temerity to preface each of these dialogues with a brief impression of the distinguished occupant of the other pulpit, with whom it was my delight and privilege to be on speaking terms of so much value and enjoyment, not only to myself, but also to many others. For this temerity, I must presume on their indulgence. These embellishments may, I hope, supply something of that dimension which has to be sacrificed in transcribing the spoken into the written word, and preserve the vibration of identity which, in whatever medium, is essential to communication.

JOSEPH MCCULLOCH
St Mary-le-Bow

The distinguished communicator who is to take part in the lunch-hour dialogue at St Mary-le-Bow arrives about noon, and has to climb three flights of stairs to our penthouse and roof-garden between the tower and the church. My first impression of Edna O'Brien, whom I met about two flights up, was that she did not climb the stairs so much as float upwards towards me like some enchanting ethereal creature from Prospero's island.

I had read her novels and seen many pictures of her, in newspapers and on television. But to convey what she is like in person needs a lyric poet of considerable quality. She is the defeat of those who struggle, as I do, to be resolutely unromantic, and to profess a sceptical attitude towards the legendary charm of the Hibernian. She has it all—the physical attributes of lovely skin, green eyes, auburn hair—what I expect Galsworthy did his best to convey of elusive beauty in the Irene of the *Forsyte Saga*, and Jung was unconsciously attempting in his various efforts to describe man's archetypal *anima*. But her most memorable attribute is a soft Irish voice of singular charm which makes a kind of music compelling you to listen when she speaks. She has no small talk with which the English are trained to disguise what they are feeling and thinking. She feels what she thinks, rather than *vice versa*. There is no mistaking that she reacts perhaps too immediately and sensitively to the crudities and cruelties of the contemporary scene.

But behind all this, there are no less unmistakably a high intelligence and acute awareness of the human drama. She knows from experience a great deal about love and life. I had feared that in the pulpit the unfamiliarity of the occasion might unnerve her. But within a few minutes, as the ensuing dialogue shows, she was herself, feeling aloud what she thought, and holding the City audience as spellbound as I have ever seen them. The soft Irish voice flowed on, and a strange beauty invaded with poetry the halting prose of our working existence. Galsworthy, Jung, you should have known Edna O'Brien!

DIALOGUE WITH

Edna O'Brien

McCulloch We have all read a great deal, not only about Edna O'Brien, but what she has written. Recently pondering on her novels, I suddenly thought that we had never talked about fear. Quite a large number of the characters in her novels—in most novels—are dominated by fear, and I suddenly realised that we were a very terrified species. Do you think we are, Edna?

O'Brien I think that at this moment it's a pertinent question! Yes I think fear is probably man's greatest handicap. We all have fear: fear of each other, fear of ourselves, fear of failure, fear of living, and of course, the middle-of-the-night fear, which is the fear of dying. I think that fear is a dreadful drawback because it stops us living in the moment. I would like to be robbed of some of my fears. Some of them were founded very much in childhood, on the fear of God and definitely the fear of hell. But along with that, we have a fear I think that we could easily live without and that is the fear of each other. I suppose it comes about because we don't really *meet* each other. One bit of us meets the other bit of the other person, but somehow we find it difficult to be our real selves with other people, and therefore we are, if not *false*, we are diminished and often artificial. And I think fear, like envy, or indeed any other vice, is an extremely contagious thing, and that we owe it to each other to say, 'Yes, you are afraid. Be less afraid!' A lot of it, I imagine, springs from childhood—perhaps parents nowadays are more understanding—but a lot of children are told not to do this or that, not to displease, not to spill, not to fall, and when you have that drummed into you day after day, you become a little fearful and hesitant. And certainly Irish Catholicism is very much founded on the stone of fear and of punishment. I don't know enough about English upbringing or religion; it seems to be a lot more reasonable.

Fear in another form can make one more sensitive. I remember once finding a wonderful quotation: 'Fear intenerates the heart, making it fit for all gracious impressions'; I looked up 'intenerates', which seemed to me a great word, and it said, 'to soften or make tender'. So that every handicap perhaps has something of value in it. I would hate to find that people were fear-*less* because it might mean they were closed.

McCULLOCH Fear, presumably, has a built-in purpose, hasn't it, in the whole human constitution?

O'BRIEN Well, yes, I suppose if one is in a jungle, one is in danger, but the difficulty is discerning when one is in a real jungle and when one is in a jungle of one's own imagining.

McCULLOCH I would say—do you agree?—that this particular generation is more frightened in many ways than any before it?

O'BRIEN No, although I would think the world *is* more frightening now because we have easier access to it. We look at television, we know what is going on in Vietnam or in Ireland or in Mongolia, and we know how much nearer the dangers are, what man has done to conquer man and to invent all the terrible weapons and strategies to maim and kill. So that it is brought to our minds more. But the younger generation, in my opinion—the ones I have met through my own children—are less frightened than my generation because they seem not to care so much about formal values—the values of material success. I feel that the phrase 'to drop out', is a lovely phrase; why not 'drop out' if one wants to? It isn't failure in human terms, only in society's terms.

McCULLOCH Yes, I have been thinking about dropping out for quite a while! But to be serious, I am profoundly interested in what you say because I think the young are showing a courage, socially, that we—that I, at least, and my lot—never showed.

O'BRIEN It is a courage and also it's a sense of proportion. I think what they have learnt is what really, in the end, matters; what is *necessary*. Most of the things we do are not necessary, perhaps even what you and I are doing now! I think to a great extent, *conversation*, too much conversation anyhow, is an agitation. I think silence—that lovely silence which isn't a strain—is a quite nice thing, and young people have that. You can see them in a room and they can be very quiet.

McCULLOCH Now Edna, have you ever lived in silence with somebody else?

O'BRIEN I am not so good at living with other people, that is one of my crosses, I was going to say failures, but we are using other symbols.

McCULLOCH I remember my wife and I, after she'd been ill, had to go down for three months to Cornwall, just to be quiet, and we had a rule of silence that we worked out together: three hours in the morning and four hours in the evening. You ask her and she will tell you about it. It worked absolutely marvellously.

O'BRIEN I think it could, if it is mutual. I was, once in my life, married to quite a dictatorial person, who used to insist on what he called 'silence periods'. Well, that made everyone hysterical. I have lived in silence, I think, with my sons, talking a bit, and listening. In the country the sounds of birds or much preferably, the sound of water and nature, make one actually hear the silence which is a beautiful thing, because it is like a hum.

McCULLOCH Now, that is interesting because I was driven away, by various people, last week, to be quiet, and I went to the country and—I won't say what I thought of the cuckoo—but the cuckoo started at four o'clock, and you can't tell me *that* is a beautiful thing. I went to the window and said 'Shut up!' It was worse than the lorries going along Cheapside! I find a lot of City men who are far less boring than the cuckoo, even though they repeat the same things and you know exactly what they are going to say next. You must admit that civilization has something to offer besides the natural world?

O'BRIEN Oh yes, but I think we need to restore ourselves frequently in the natural world in order to become fully conscious for the other world. What happens is that one gets inundated, by things, and life tends to become automatic. I am reading, at the moment, Maurice Nicoll; he worked with Jung. One of the things he says above all else is to wait for a moment to receive incoming impressions, not to rush at it, to wait. And in order to develop that habit, one has to, sometimes, get away from the craziness, you know. You can't be in a fun-fair all the time. But I don't, on the other hand, think it is good to become a beautiful, lofty-minded hermit, because that is very confined. Ideally, I would love to divide my life, but then I think, so would everyone. For instance, we might try to emulate what they do in China. I don't know modern China, but there is one thing that Mao Tse Tung has done, which is to alter people's functions: a writer might have to work in the fields for three months, and a farmer or a field-worker, in a factory. I hate to admit publicly that I would like to be forced, because I am always resisting force, but I would like, to a certain extent, to be *nudged* into doing other things.

McCulloch Edna, may we go back for a moment to what we were talking about earlier on? You spoke of fear: of yourself, and of others, but what you never mentioned was fear *for* yourself, and *for* others.

O'Brien Ah, well, it is very interesting, but usually a person who has fear *of* doesn't have fear *for*. I think I have fear for my children but I have no fear of them. Fear *for* someone, isn't so much fear as a great love, and a great concern that they shall walk well. There is a poem of Yeats about love and he says

A pity beyond all telling
Is hid in the heart of love,
The folks who are buying and selling,
The clouds on their journey above,
These, and the cold, wet winds
Pity the one I love.

I can't remember it all, but it is mainly hoping against hope that the person who is beloved will be all right, and will walk safely through life.

I think if I were born again I would ask to be born into a different environment, where the dark and the ghosts and the devil, and for that matter, God, and many other things, were talked about in a reasonable way. Coming from the west of Ireland, although it was abundantly fertile and lovely and, as a writer, I am grateful for it, it was also submerged in a mass of ignorance, and superstition and a lack of clarity. Because what makes us so afraid is the thing we half see, or half hear, as in a wood at dusk, when a tree stump becomes an animal and a sound becomes a siren. And most of that fear is the fear of not knowing, of not actually seeing correctly. I would love to have new eyes. My last book was called *Night* and it ended by saying: 'Oh, star of the morning, oh, slippery path, oh, guardian angel of mortals, give us eyes, lend us a hand, lead us to the higher shores of golden, incandescent love.'

McCulloch That's beautiful! I suppose the whole secret of life is imagination, isn't it?

O'Brien Well, I often debate about this. When I read Proust and the great writers, I realize that imagination is the greatest thing in the world. When I read Maurice Nicoll and the Buddhist mystics and children's essays, I realize that imagination breeds a lot of pain.

McCulloch Of course it does. The Hebrews from the very beginning ruled that imagination was the clue. They said that the fall of man was due to an evil imagination which came into the world.

But to go back to what you were saying about religion in Ireland in the early days, surely the danger was, that there was an attempt on the part of religion to make you love by fear. Now, can you love by fear?

O'BRIEN No. Fear puts love out the window. I think the moment one does love—really love—not asking for anything back, that fear would go then. It would be a sort of purging of the imagination. I think that people are born with the innate sense of purity about who or what they like or don't like, and that gets lost through indoctrination. The indoctrination is what is destructive. I think the greatest thing you can teach children is a sense of themselves and of what is right and wrong and to think for themselves.

McCULLOCH I would teach children what makes them free and what doesn't. I am not interested in what is right and wrong, I think moralising is bad.

O'BRIEN When I said right and wrong, I meant from the point of view, not of laws or morality, but of knowing that if they go out and chop down a tree or a person, then that is something which will cause them to suffer.

McCULLOCH Well, isn't it—to put it again quite clearly—a matter of what ties us up ultimately? How do we get tied up? Because most people in adult life *are* tied up, aren't they? They are not free.

O'BRIEN Oh, and tied up is a lovely way of putting it. They certainly are.

McCULLOCH I don't mean in marriage.

O'BRIEN I wasn't thinking of that. I was thinking that there are a lot of different ways of losing freedom. Earning our living seems to constitute a great part of our lives and it is a big bloody bore. Wondering who loves us gets us knotted up, then as time goes on, houses and all that—keeping up appearances. Until a man or a woman is like an old horse, weighed down with all these things, and of course, when we look at our children or our grandchildren, *they* seem free because they have not actually grasped yet what their lives, roughly, will be about.

There is a wonderful thing that Camus said: 'Once you become a fully conscious man, you can never be totally, blissfully, properly happy'. And then, as one gets older, one becomes aware of the *world*. You know—'... for whom the bell tolls, it tolls for thee'. I think individual happiness is really out of the question then, because although one might be relatively happy in one's own life, people require so much of us, more than we can actually give, and we don't know quite what to do about it. I think one of the most important things (in cities particularly), that one could give to one's neighbour—funnily enough, it is very simple—is time.

McCulloch Yes! Now, I was listening to you just now talking about the world, but I am profoundly convinced that there are two worlds. We live in both; we are amphibious and the whole problem of what is called 'happiness' is making some kind of balance between the two worlds.

O'Brien Do you mean the interior world and the exterior?

McCulloch Yes. The outside world, in which you can make very little headway—the more you live the more you realise that your shoving doesn't move the elephant very much—and the powerful and far greater world within, the world of the mind and the spirit in which you move and in which there is real freedom from fear.

O'Brien I agree that the interior world is, in a way, the most valued and valuable, for that matter, the most resident world, because we are all alone there with our thoughts.

McCulloch No, I don't think I am *alone* with my thoughts, I am alone with my God, which is much more important.

O'Brien I think if one was with one's God, one would not be alone at all. So that when you say you are alone with your God, you are alone with yourself, beholden to your God.

I vacillate between states of certain love towards people, and paranoia. The times in my life when I have really been with another human being—a man or a woman or a child—and I have really looked at their faces and their necks and their eyelids and their whole being and what their faces say, apart from what their lips are saying, and have observed myself observing that state—I have, at those odd and very, very rare moments, felt that it is really possible to be very near another person. And there is then an extraordinary—it is very subtle—but an extraordinary kind of glory.

Now, when one talks of God, it is very often (in my case, anyhow), a longing and a desire for God rather than pure faith. So that when you say you are alone with God, I think that I have not come to that yet because I am perhaps too caught up in the exacting God that I was breast-fed on, which is a different God, really I think, from yours. One of the things I love about growing older is how much more—not comprehensible life is—but how much more mysterious the possibilities are. I was in a taxi recently, and the taxi-driver said that he wished he was thirty again, and I said, 'Oh God, I don't wish I was thirty, not again'. Not because of any kind of sourness of not wanting to relive my life, but because I feel that whatever the journey it is that one is on, the longer you are on it the more chance you have to reach—I can't call it destination—but some kind of light. I don't mean to sound pompous about that, because it is a very fragile feeling. But I have it increasingly, and I find everything more interesting and more fresh, and more to be looked at. And more awful things too. The task is to accept both.

McCULLOCH Is life more beautiful as you grow older?

O'BRIEN Life is not so much more beautiful, as that one has a greater interest in it. When you are younger, you are more wrapped up in yourself, and that is very nice. But growing old—I think a lot of assistance comes to one, you know.

McCULLOCH That is a beautiful statement. I think it is true. I think what dominates human life is a struggle between love and fear, and that as you grow older, the meaning of love gets clearer and you triumph over the fear.

O'BRIEN Well, ideally, that would be nice. Fear is quite a devil, you know. It is quite hard to step on. I think that it can be lessened. One wouldn't want to wipe it out altogether. I think we are all stuck with it, but—I hate to sound suddenly practical—a lot of it is to do with breathing, with just breathing in and out, and taking everything slower, not out of fatigue but out of the fact that every minute is itself, and it is good to live that minute. And it is good to pause.

22 May 1973

Bernard always ascends the stairs two at a time, and is with us before I have descended one flight to meet him. The zestful agility and swift arrival are characteristic of him no less mentally than physically. You have to move quickly to keep up with him, whether you read him or talk with him—an exhilarating experience, even though at times you are faint but pursuing. He is so very much alive that he cannot help communicating life, especially that of the mind.

He is merciless towards cant, jargon, humbug or any professional obscurantism. Those, and they are very many, who have seen him only engaged in controversy on television or read him only in pungent articles when he does not spare to smite, get the impression that he is always formidable and ruthless, lacking the milk of human kindness and the honey of social graces. Nothing could be more untrue. In person, he is the very reverse, eminently sensitive and courteous and unfailingly kind. I know nobody more entertaining as a guest or more delightful to entertain. I would estimate that Bernard Levin has piled up a considerable credit score for the number of times he has bitten his tongue and refrained from speaking when it might cause hurt. Allowing for the swiftness of his mental processes and the difficult of suffering fools gladly, this must mean a quantity of marks in his favour. But when he has joined combat, he wields the sharpest of swords, as potentates, premiers and plenipotentiaries galore could testify. My guess is that, as a child, his chief delight was pricking balloons with a darning-needle. He has grown up to be one of the most fearless and accomplished critical essayists extant.

His annual occupation of the visitor's pulpit in St Mary-le-Bow, is an event enthusiastically appreciated in the City. On the first occasion ten years ago, he described the experience in his press column the next day: 'As for the pulpit,' he concluded, 'no home should be without one.' O rare Bernard Levin!

DIALOGUE WITH

Bernard Levin

McCULLOCH The last time Mr Levin was here, we discussed, straightforwardly, the whole ground of belief, or non-belief, in God. At the end of that dialogue I fired at him a question, 'In view of all that we've been saying, do you despair of man?', and to my amazement he replied, 'No, I don't, because I believe that the deepest thing in man is altruism'. Mr Levin, do you still hold that position?

LEVIN Well, I do, though I must say, however, that I've never claimed the virtue of consistency, and my text is Walt Whitman's, 'Do I contradict myself? Very well then, I contradict myself. I am large, I contain multitudes.' However, I still do believe what I said then, that the deepest thing in man is altruism. 'Deepest' is, in fact, a rather happily chosen word, because I didn't say 'the universal thing'—it manifestly isn't—but the deepest thing, arguably the most fundamental thing, on which, ultimately, I believe it possible man rests. Yes, I do still believe that.

McCULLOCH But in view of the fact that man is a creature of evolution, might not that appear to be a contradiction in terms? Quite clearly it has been the selfish desire to survive which has brought man where he is.

LEVIN I agree with that, but I don't see why any contradiction arises. After all, when I say the deepest thing in man is altruism, I am not thinking of the slow struggles over the evolutionary ages. I am not thinking of the Pithecanthropus, or indeed the early forms of life on this planet. I am thinking of man as we know him today.

McCULLOCH But surely, man today doesn't seem to have altered very greatly. I mean the very nature of our society is red in tooth and claw, isn't it?

LEVIN Now I am glad you said that, because this is, in fact, what I have against your case. It is indeed *apparently* true, if we look around us at the present age, and in the immediately preceding ages, that man is red in tooth and claw, and behaves in an extremely beastly fashion, very much of the time, but I am amazed that you should have the nerve to offer that as an argument against me. I believe that man is basically good, *basically* good, I say, even though this goodness is frequently distorted and imperfect. But that's as far as I will go. Whereas you believe, in fact, that the universe is ordered by a divine being who is entirely good, and who is, indeed, a definition of goodness, love and perfection, and then you ask me if I don't think there is some contradiction in my belief in the goodness of man and the badness of the world. Don't you believe there is some contradiction in the goodness of *your* God, and the badness of the world?

McCulloch H'm, I can see us getting bogged down in that one! Can we get back to the main topic which we've been discussing? I'd like to pursue it further. You have produced the idea that here is a creature who has managed to get where he has got by putting number one first and foremost; you then advance the proposition that the only way in which he can survive now is that he should put the other person first and foremost.

Levin That, in fact, roughly speaking, *is* my position, and I argue it thus: that altruism is a higher form of existence than selfishness, and this, after all, is the definition of evolution—a progress from a lower to a higher form of existence. And I think that when altruism first emerged in man, he had moved onto a higher plane. I think we have got to the point now where altruism, in some form, is man's salvation.

McCulloch This raises some enormous questions. It means that man in the twentieth century must go back upon the whole of his past in some way, or not go back upon, but transcend.

Levin Well, man's whole history is a history of going back upon, or transcending his past. We abandon superstitions, certain modes of living, certain cruelties. I don't know if we find enough to substitute for them, but we do, slowly, through the ages, transcend man's earlier and more primitive nature.

McCulloch I agree, he is slowly abandoning certain obvious forms of selfishness, but he still goes on with his capitalist society, doesn't he?

Levin Yes, but I don't see what is wrong with that either. I am not one of those who believes that capitalism is in some sense intrinsically wicked, whatever excesses it may, in fact, give rise to.

McCulloch But in terms of altruism, it must be so, because if I am altruistic then the nature of my society must be a co-operation with others, not a competition with them.

LEVIN Yes, but that implies that man must be either wholly selfish or wholly altruistic. I don't believe that is so. There are certain saints, no doubt, who are wholly altruistic; there are a rather more numerous band of people who are wholly selfish; but I believe that both elements, not only can, but do, and perhaps should, commingle in man's nature.

McCULLOCH But would you say that you are more yourself if you achieve altruism?

LEVIN I didn't say that I was more myself, I implied that perhaps it would be a more satisfactory basis to life. It is more blessed to give than to receive, if I might remind you.

McCULLOCH Well, I believe that I have heard that somewhere. How does the whole question of one's duty to oneself square with altruism? If indeed altruism is the better self, or a better basis for society, is there nothing that I owe myself?

LEVIN Yes, one has a duty to oneself. One has also a duty to other people. I think it is impossible to lay down lines by which one may define which is which, and indeed, which is more important at any given moment. The boundaries in your case might well be different from the boundaries in mine. But again, you are making the two things mutually exclusive, which I don't think they are. We *do* have a duty both to ourselves and to others. In a certain sense, of course, they are the same. If I may just elaborate on this point for a moment: I don't believe that a man can live at the highest possible level for himself, if he does leave out of account his duty to others, and solely lives for himself. I think that is an unsatisfactory kind of living, though goodness knows, most of us live it a lot of the time.

McCULLOCH But the whole basis of the argument must rest, I would have thought, upon some deeper centre to the whole fabric of existence?

LEVIN Now, here we come to what may, in fact, be the only real, basic difference between us, which is where we respectively derive our beliefs in our particular forms of altruism. I do not derive mine from any external inspiration, and presumably a Christian does. I don't see that this, in fact, solves the problem. I don't see why it makes more sense to say, as you do: I believe that the purpose—the centre, as you call it—is God, and to say, as I do: I do not believe there is any such centre.

McCulloch Well, I don't suppose the word 'centre' is perhaps the best one. But I must look for some unifying principle, otherwise I do not see that life can make any sense at all, or that any moral categories can be really authoritative upon me.

Levin But then, how do you account for the fact that life *does* make a great deal of sense to me, unless you are going to say that I am deluding myself, which you may well say?

McCulloch That is the whole purpose of this dialogue—to find out! I still find it very difficult to see what moral 'oughts' you can impose upon yourself, unless you use the word 'external'. Incidentally, I don't like that word, but I admit that the idea of God has been externalized, though it is, I think, a false idea of God. But I am profoundly convinced that there must be some purpose implicit in evolution. I cannot, in the midst of this evolutionary process, find any kind of landmark or guideline unless I am able to understand somewhere a unifying principle that is being worked out in it.

Levin I am tempted to reply simply, 'I'm sorry if you can't, because I can'. I don't see that there is any need to say that there is a purpose, over and above man's purpose. For instance, if you make it entirely personal, the most personal thing inside us is conscience. There *is* that, I believe, in all of us, deeply buried sometimes and overlaid with all sorts of selfishness and everything else. But I believe that a man knows, unless he be actually deranged, that he is doing wrong, even if that knowledge doesn't stop him doing it. I don't see any need to postulate any kind of God to instil that into mankind, any more than I feel a need for any kind of God to explain why one man's eyes are blue and another's brown. This is in man. Now how it got there—you might ask similarly how our bodies got the way they are; they got that way through evolution. *You* can say, if you like, that God pressed the initial button; I just don't think it necessary to say that. But if this is the only difference in the end between us, it is a very small one to make the great divide out of.

McCulloch Now this is very interesting, because you obviously see man as an answer. I only see him as a question. To my mind, the whole thing is raising the question all the time, of meaning, of purpose, and so on. You seem to find the answer already there, and I'm puzzled to know how you do that.

Levin I only find the answer in the sense that I don't believe man needs anything but himself and his world to carry out his purposes. Now what I do believe is that through evolution, not in the Darwinian, biological sense, but in the social sense, mankind is very slowly, and with a large number of steps backward, improving his lot. I believe this to be so, not on mystical grounds, or on grounds of faith, but on the evidence of what I can see, crude and imperfect though it be. I don't feel the need for anything more than that. Why should you?

McCULLOCH Well, at some point one has to say, surely, 'Here am I, a curious, freak creature, obviously unlike all the other creatures, in that I am sensitive and, to a certain extent, intelligent, but I am to assume that I can be this in a kind of doltish universe, a universe that has no meaning'.

LEVIN I don't think the universe *is* doltish. I think a number of things that go on in it are doltish, but on balance it seems to me that very slowly, undoltishness is getting the upper hand, and a good thing too. But I don't see why the fact that I don't believe that the universe is directed to a particular aim by something outside the universe, or independent from the universe, means that it has no purpose, no meaning or no sense. All I am saying is that it derives it from itself.

McCULLOCH Therefore, you would say that the human kind of intelligence, is a freakish by-product?

LEVIN It's as much a by-product as any other development of evolution. After all, I am not going to pretend that the central mystery of where the world came from, or where life and consciousness came from, is not a mystery to me. It *is* a mystery to me. All I am saying is that it becomes no less of a mystery if you smile and say, 'God arranged it so'. That doesn't seem to do anything but shift the argument one step further back.

McCULLOCH I agree about shifting the argument one step further back. But you have in you a desire to reason the thing; you must have. Here is an extraordinary situation in which you find yourself, and willy-nilly you are driven to try to form for yourself a reasonable idea of the context in which you are situated.

LEVIN I do indeed. But this is the only world I know, the only *universe* I know; moreover, it's the only universe I feel any need for, and goodness knows we have got enough to do in it without seeking for explanations outside it.

McCULLOCH You are still talking about God as externalized, and assuming that *I* externalize God. This is not true. The God that we worship—in this church—is in the midst of us. We don't go to him as though he were outside us but as though we moved and lived and were, in his being.

LEVIN What I think you are saying is that God is within all of us. I said, five minutes ago, conscience is within all of us. If you mean no more than that by God, I am prepared to go along with you and there is no disagreement between us. But you must, presumably, mean more than that.

McCULLOCH I do mean more than that. You said at the beginning that the deepest thing in man is altruism, I say that the deepest thing in man is God. I would say that that is *why* the deepest thing in man is altruism.

LEVIN But I can't see God, and I can see altruism.

McCULLOCH I don't think you need bother about *seeing* God. You need not bother about the senses at all in this context. I would say that when man experiences this determination to give himself for others, he is then moving at the very deepest level of his consciousness, where God moves 'in the deep and dazzling darkness', as Henry Vaughan put it.

LEVIN What you're saying is, 'God moves in a mysterious way, his wonders to perform'. You always fall back on that in the end. This seems to me to be wholly unsatisfactory as an explanation of his inactivity.

McCULLOCH And yet it would seem to accord with your own position, where you began by accepting that this is a mystery. All you would not go on to say was, 'There must be some Being behind the mystery'.

LEVIN I accept that it is a mystery in the sense that we do not know, and possibly never will know, *everything* about ourselves and the universe. I accept that. All I am saying is that *you* are not helping me to solve it.

McCULLOCH I must apologise for that. But I want to know—to return to our opening gambit—upon what *do* you really base your present hope for the future of man. You say that we are getting better and better, you almost produced a doctrine of progress, to my astonishment.

LEVIN I am, in fact, old-fashioned enough to believe in the doctrine of progress, which I think has been too readily abandoned in the modern world, but I believe—well, I will answer your question.

I base it, first, obviously, on a kind of instinctive optimism which I believe is in all men and is the thing which protects them from despair, but that, in itself, wouldn't be satisfactory to me. I base it on the fact that the world seems to me to progress, despite all the wickedness and cruelty and poverty, in a kind of three-steps-forward-two-steps-back method. And it does seem to me that there is more altruism in the world today, even if we take it at the simplest and most practical level of wealthy nations helping economically poor nations. Now there are great problems and difficulties in that and great imperfections in the way it is done, nevertheless it *is* done on a scale today that is unique or unprecedented in human history. That to me is a very important thing. And such things as the discoveries of science in combating disease; in discovering the causes of disease; in social organisation—I believe in fact, very slowly, man's social and indeed, political organisation is improving over the world.

These are all signs, only signs I grant you, they are not proof, that the universe slowly, and with much stumbling and fumbling, gets a better place to live in and allows mankind to live more fully, and higher up the scale of his own nature, than before. It is on this that I base my belief that this will go on happening, and if I am extinguished by an atom bomb tomorrow, I may well have been proved wrong.

22 November 1966

Kenneth Clark is a kind of Olympian figure. I did originally imagine that this view of him was perhaps peculiar to myself. But on the first occasion he came to do a dialogue, as my wife was abroad, I took him to lunch at the Garrick, where the members clearly showed that they shared my sentiment of respect towards him, almost reverence. This, I think, is simply because in a society which shows many symptoms of a relapse into barbarism, one who can play his distinguished part in such a world and yet remain not of it, has manifestly achieved an integrity where many feel that they most betray themselves.

There is nothing new about the tendency to give approval to the better things and yet pursue the worse. What is new in our own age is our immensely increased facility to purvey the worse so that the better is lost to sight. We have acquired the most powerful of engines to vulgarise the imagination of man, and blur his judgement of what is true or false, beautiful or ugly, good or bad. But the approval of the better is in our nature, however it may be suppressed. It was for that reason that a television series by a man long distinguished in the field of arts was watched with wonder and delighted appreciation by a vast number of viewers. His subject was *Civilization.* It was thus that Kenneth Clark became admired and needed not only as an eminent authority in a particular field of knowledge but also as a communicator of the values which rescue man from barbarism, and essentially distinguish him from the brutes that perish. He had been invited by the B.B.C. to talk on a subject to which he had devoted himself throughout his life, and on which he would have talked with the same erudite competence whether his audience had been fifty or five millions. It so happened that he gave many what they had most long needed—the renewal of confidence in the meaning of humanity. Though Lord Clark would probably disclaim it at once, he did that because he himself is an eminently civilized person.

DIALOGUE WITH

Kenneth Clark

McCulloch I want to ask some questions arising from what the B.B.C. says is the most impressive series they have ever had—that on *Civilization* which you gave. Lord Clark, you said in that series that you could recognize civilization when you saw it but you could not define it yet. You mentioned various attributes or qualities which are essential in civilization: confidence, energy, will, creative power, a sense of permanence, and so on. Do you think our Western society has enough of these essential qualities to prevent our civilization going into a decline?

Clark I ought to say that when I started that series on *Civilization* I didn't really know what was going to happen by the time I got to the thirteenth programme. All I knew for certain was that no *a priori* definition of civilization was going to work. I thought that civilization, as Goethe said, was one of those organic things which could only be defined in its growth, and all I did in that first programme was to give the kind of prerequisite of a civilized country or society, in the same way that one says that a tree, in order to grow, must have a certain amount of moisture, depth of soil, and so on. I did not mean, of course, to limit a definition of civilization to those qualities of confidence, energy, will and so forth, and as the series went on, I hoped to find, and I did in fact find, new discoveries, new enlargements of the human mind taking place. First, there was the flowering of courtesy and chivalry in the twelfth century, then the enlargement of reason in the seventeenth century, the idea of natural law, all the ideas of the Enlightenment, the idea of tolerance, the love of nature and, finally, the humanitarian idea which played such a great part in the nineteenth century and still does today.

Now you ask me what we have today. We certainly have energy and will, of that there is no doubt. There may be no point at all in sending man to the moon, but it is an extraordinary proof of the energy of our present time. We are not going just to disintegrate or liquefy, the way the late antique civilization did. We have creative power in a technical sense but we do lack a sense of permanence.

This is something that has overcome us in the last few years, and is a very serious matter. I am also rather inclined to think that we are losing confidence. It seems incredible that the Americans, with their vast resources and their wonderful fund of goodwill, should be losing confidence, but that is the situation they have been in for the last few years.

So that I would say, from the point of view of energy, creativeness, will, we are all right. As to the other things I have mentioned, that have accrued to civilization in the course of its growth—that is to say, courtesy, the rule of law, the rule of reason, toleration, the love of nature—all those have probably declined and the only one that still holds up is humanitarianism.

McCULLOCH And may I ask a subsidiary question? Where, in the world at the moment, do you see civilization as having its strongest hold?

CLARK By the last word I spoke, by humanitarianism. I believe the thought and the care that we feel for other people—which God knows is inadequate—is infinitely stronger than it has ever been among the mass of people all over the world. This concern, which, I should add, has been enormously enhanced and made vivid by the medium of television, I believe to be something really living, and an advance on anything we have had. And I think it has gone hand in hand with a real growth in the belief in love as the prime mover of human life. So, thus far, I think we have got something to go on.

McCULLOCH Do you think it is possible for a mass industrial society to produce great works of art, or does art depend, for its vitality, upon smaller structures, such as were there in ancient Greece or medieval Italy?

CLARK I think one must distinguish between art that is created by the individual mind, or under the rules of an individual mind, and art that is created by a group of people. That is almost a distinction between art and craftmanship. That one will get, under present conditions, the kind of art that created a Cotswold village or a small Italian town, is unthinkable. Those were the creation of what you might call a 'craft society'. On the other hand, the creation of great works of art by individuals arose in the Renaissance, and continued into the nineteenth century, when the individual artist was entirely remote from society. It is a great mistake to think that the artist must be completely involved in society. The great artists of the nineteenth century—obviously Cézanne, but to a lesser degree all the Impressionists, Manet, Gauguin, and so forth—were all removed from the society of their time and produced great works of art as individuals.

McCulloch You know, there is something which I think a lot of us are bothered about at the moment and that is, how do you see the probable effect upon our art and our general ethos and way of life, of entering this European adventure?

Clark Well, I don't think it will make any difference at all because if art is in a healthy condition it has no boundaries. I said several times, in the *Civilization* series that the great periods of art have been international periods. This is absolutely true. The three epochs of Gothic art were all international; the great period of the Baroque was international, Rococo was international—at least one can say, if it didn't touch a country, that country was the poorer. And therefore I do not think that our entry into Europe will make any difference, but if it did, it would be to our advantage. You must remember a time—*I* can remember a time—just after World War I, when there was not a single painting by Cézanne in England; there were a few in Wales. When the Matisses were shown in 1920, that was the first time the name of Matisse had ever been heard of. We were absolutely cut off; cut off, by the way, by the prejudices of the Directors of the Tate and the leading critics of the time—except of course, Roger Fry—and that did us no good at all; our own art became provincial, feeble, and almost entirely expendable.

McCulloch It is cheering to hear such a positive reaction!

Now, at the end of this very great series you quoted something from Yeats. May I read it?

> Things fall apart; the centre cannot hold;
> Mere anarchy is loosed upon the world,
> The blood-dimmed tide is loosed, and everywhere
> The ceremony of innocence is drowned;
> The best lack all conviction, while the worst
> Are full of passionate intensity.

And you went on to say, the trouble is we still have no centre. Do you think that a central faith of some kind is essential for civilization?

Clark The short answer is, yes. But I would need great latitude in defining the words, 'a central faith'. I would also need to say that a central faith can exist and *not* produce a civilization, because the central faith of Islam has been incredibly consistent for—whatever it is—1,300 years, and has produced only intermittent periods of civilization. So that, although I think the central faith is necessary, it does not automatically produce a civilization.

But when I say, 'the centre will not hold', Mr Yeats said, '*the* centre'; and there has only once in European history been '*the* centre' and that was in the Catholic Middle Ages from the tenth or eleventh to the first quarter of the fourteenth century, when the thing began to break up. That period, though it left a legacy of fear and cruelty and many other terrible things, was one of the great moments in human existence.

But there have been other centres since then: the belief in reason; the belief in cause and effect; in mathematics, which dominated seventeenth century thought; in natural law, which is perhaps as unfounded as Christian belief but which satisfied a number of non-Christians; the belief in permanence—that things which are made to last are more valuable than things which can be thrown away; and the belief in the possibility of perfection. Now these are great beliefs which have sustained the world—even until quite recently. One of the latest to go is the belief that things made to last are more valuable than things that are thrown away, and now artists or art critics, who wish to think that they are being clever, say that *art* should not be made to last, that it should only give a moment's satisfaction. And this joins up with the lowest form of philosophy—the philosophy of immediate sensation. That, I think, is a real loss of a centre. The belief in reason, of course, has long ago been abandoned. The great Enlightenment, and the belief, from Voltaire onwards, in toleration—all these beliefs have been disappearing. From that point of view, I think, we are in a bad way.

McCulloch And this beautiful phrase that the poet uses, 'The ceremony of innocence is drowned'. Had you in mind, when you quoted it, that the permissive society had blown that out too?

Clark I don't think I had it directly in mind but I always was very much impressed by the way that Mr Yeats related 'innocence' to 'ceremony'. We had the privilege of knowing him and I remember his reading to us his poem to his daughter in which he says, 'And may her bridegroom bring her to a house where all's accustomed, ceremonious,/For arrogance and hatred are the wares peddled in the thoroughfares'. And this feeling, that we somehow maintain our innocence through ceremony, tradition, courtesy, though I wouldn't like to give a rational justification of it, I believe to be profoundly true.

McCulloch Thank you for that answer which strikes me with a peculiar freshness. This is something I, for one, and I daresay others here, have never seriously thought about. It opens up an interesting field for further exploration.

Now I think something we would all like to be enlightened on is how does one recognize a great work of art? There seems to be a general consensus about past works of genius, but does that give us criteria for judging contemporary works?

Clark These are two questions. The first one is, how does one recognize a great work of art? The answer is, ultimately, only by intuition, there is no other way. But that intuition must be educated by experience, it must be related to what other people have felt; the merely self-satisfied, arrogant intuition will not give people a true range of understanding of art. And when I say 'educated', what can I mean except that one must believe, before one can understand? One must believe that Giotto, Donatello, Rembrandt—whoever it may be—are great artists even before one can fully appreciate them. And one must go on looking until, without any stretching of one's faculties, these great artists do appeal to one, do give one the feeling that they have given to all lovers of art in the past. In fact, one must have confidence in the critical judgements of the past, and with that precedent to sharpen, mould, educate one's intuitions, one can form a basis of aesthetic judgement. But it is not altogether easy. I mean, it does involve a lot of looking, a lot of thinking and a frequent return to the originals.

Now, the second part of your question is, can this be applied to modern art? Well, I don't for a moment deny that art since 1918 or 1916 has become something extremely different from what it was, but I do not believe that it is *fundamentally* different. My reason for that is that the moment I look at the work of some of the abstract artists, give it attention and concentrate on it, and try to see the way in which their work has developed—the moment I do that, I see that they are great artists. I give only one instance—that of Mondrian. No artist has been more totally abstract than Mondrian, but I am absolutely sure that he is a great artist. I can't, of course, use the kind of analytic-descriptive means of justifying my belief that I could in front of a Poussin, but even so, that doesn't really put me out very much because I think all analytic-descriptive justifications of one's enjoyment of a work of art are really just a load of nonsense. You could do a very good justificatory piece of prose about a very second-rate work of art.

McCulloch This question is one of those 'which-came-first-the-hen-or-the-egg' things: does the artist, in any age, merely reflect the contemporary mood, or does he, in fact, create it?

Clark I will try to answer that shortly. All great art is prophetic; there is practically no exception to that. The great artist's work is sometimes only a few years ahead of what everyone else is going to feel, or what is going to happen in the world, and sometimes it is a long way ahead. He does not create the mood that follows it, he catches it out of the air before it has actually become embodied. I'll give you an example: Picasso of the early Cubist movement produced the pictures based on straight lines and cubes and that sort of thing, *before* modern architecture began doing the same thing. The use of steel as a dominant force in architecture came after the inventions, first of all, of Picasso and then, of course, of Mondrian and the other abstract artists. The artist was prophetic, the general application followed.

McCulloch And finally, this is a question which obviously needs an hour, so if you could answer it, Lord Clark, in about two minutes! How does one explain period style—I mean, the kind of elongated lines in the early English style, the blunt, squarish look in the early sixteenth century, and so on? There *is* a period style that one can recognize, is there not?

Clark That would indeed take an hour to answer thoroughly, but I will give you a short answer. Great changes of style take place, first of all, in a few great buildings or great works of art, and are probably the result of an individual of genius responding to some spiritual need of the time. The example you give is a very correct one, the example of Gothic. Let us take the Gothic arch as created by the Abbot Suger who built Saint-Denis. He wasn't doing it in response to an engineering problem; he was doing it because that particular shape fulfilled some real spiritual need. Having created that shape, it then diffused itself from this one centre into the decorative arts, and so finally everything became Gothic in shape, you see, even down to the shoes, those long, tapering shoes of the fourteenth century.

Now rather the same thing happened at the time of the Renaissance. There was a reaction *against* the pointed arch and a reintroduction of Classic architecture. Things became square. And so one can say that the first revivers of Classical architecture were the original inventors of Renaissance style, and that the decorators, the fashion men, were taking those rhythms from a larger art.

I just ought to add, perhaps, that fashion has its own internal laws which are a sort of action-reaction movement—something which is outside the main laws of art history and constitutes a problem of its own.

McCULLOCH Could you help us to identify any one style as indicative or characteristic of our own age?

CLARK Well, in a way, I have answered that already because, undoubtedly, what we may call the 'steel girder style' is the style of our own age.

McCULLOCH But you must admit that the women walking along Cheapside aren't quite looking like steel girders!

CLARK Oh, no no no. It hasn't spread to fashion, I quite agree! It's too difficult. But the steel girder style, as it were—originally the Mondrian style—is the dominant style of our age and has influenced the design of radios and transistors and refrigerators—everything. It *hasn't* yet spread, I am glad to say, to the ladies of Cheapside!

3 August 1971

If we needed evidence that there is an unequal distribution of natural gifts, an actress might well ask why should a woman who is capable of becoming a Cabinet Minister be also endowed with one of the most beautiful speaking voices to be heard on or off stage. Perhaps the members of the Opposition have been warned, like Odysseus and his sailors, to beware of the siren's music.

It remains a fact that so attractive a person is also a dedicated and exceptionally able politician who eschews most of the tricks of the trade, as well as those of her sex, and applies her well-furnished and disciplined mind to elucidating the facts of our confused situation. Shirley seems to me to show much the same down-to-earth attitude to life as Browning's Bishop Blougram.

> The common problem, yours, mine, everyone's,
> Is not to fancy what were fair in life
> Provided it could be,—but, finding first
> What may be, then find how to make it fair
> Up to our means—a very different thing!
> No abstract intellectual plan of life
> Quite irrespective of life's plainest laws,
> But one, a man, who is man and nothing more,
> May lead within a world which (by your leave)
> Is Rome or London—not Fool's paradise.

There is no mistaking that for Shirley Williams politics is a vocation rather than a career. This has meant that, though she by no means scorns delights, she has to live laborious days. The more difficult and arduous the demands upon her, the greater the zest with which she gives of herself. Admittedly, she has a job which extends her to the full and provides endless scope for her gifts. But had her lot been cast in a less exalted sphere of work, she would have been very much the same—just as attractive a person and with no less sense of vocation.

DIALOGUE WITH

Shirley Williams

McCulloch When I wrote to Mrs Shirley Williams in the autumn and asked if she would delight us again in the City, I said, 'It would be so good for you to get away from politics and talk about human life for a little while'. I didn't know, obviously, that immediate politics would be so pressing on this date, and it is wonderful of her to have kept her promise to come, despite her incredibly busy life at the moment.

Let me plunge in straight away and tell you what I really wanted to talk about. This is obviously a creative period in history, although everyone is pulling long faces. People are feeling after something very important, it seems to me, and great changes are taking place, which we don't yet fully understand. There was one thing that happened in this curious election [February 1974] that puzzles me, and that is that so few women Members were returned to the House of Commons. This is very strange because, of all the great changes in this century, clearly the position of woman is the most important of those changes. Does this worry you—that so few women were returned, I mean?

Williams Well, I think it is a very interesting question, because one of the great changes we are seeing in society at the present time is, as you say, the emergence of women into more of a general equality. I suspect that if this process goes on, we will have in the end a much easier and more relaxed relationship between men and women, both personally and collectively. And yet it is odd that when one has said that and when one recognizes that the impact of women on politics has been profound—you have only to think of such matters as education, health, and social services, and now consumerism, all of which used to be called, in a slightly dismissive tone, 'women's subjects' and which are now almost the centrepiece of politics—yet in spite of all that, so few women are actually involved in the activity of making decisions. The leaders of our country are *still* overwhelmingly masculine in every sphere you look at: industry, trades unions, politics, the Judiciary, everywhere. I think it is because our society, while willing to make room for women, is not willing to make changes for them. By changes, I really mean that institutions like the House of Commons sooner or later will have to adapt themselves to the fact that most women lead two lives—one as wife and mother and the other in terms of a career. At the moment this hasn't happened, and there aren't all that many women who are willing so completely to force the pattern of their lives into what is, essentially, the masculine shape of our institutions.

McCULLOCH But I wondered whether it was politics itself—I mean, there are plenty of women in other professions.

WILLIAMS Not really. I gave you the example of the Judiciary but I could give you many others. There are virtually no women in top management in Britain nor among the leaders on the General Council of the T.U.C. No, it is not unique to politics, in fact one has to say about politics that the record is marginally better than in other professions.

McCULLOCH I suppose I was thinking of women doctors, chiefly, and I was going to suggest that politics, like medicine, seems to me to be the most likely field for women's talents or gifts, if you are going to distinguish between women and men as to gifts and abilities.

WILLIAMS Well, I guess I'm not really. I think the best institutions are those which have both men and women in them. I am one of those people who quite deeply believes that most of us have the characteristics of each sex, in lesser or greater part, in ourselves and that it is nonsense to try to see men and women as being totally different, or as having characteristics which are either peculiarly feminine or peculiarly masculine. There is gentleness and tenderness in men, and I know perfectly well that there is a great deal of toughness and aggression in women, but the contribution that each can make is a bit different, because I think we do look at the world, not from the point view so much of different virtues, as of rather different preoccupations. Now the difficulty with politics, in which women can make a great contribution, is that there are not enough of us, so we are a bit odd. If you are a woman in politics, what you say interests the media much more than if you are a man, simply because you are a *woman*, and not because you are brighter or more interesting.

McCULLOCH But the different preoccupations, Shirley, are important, aren't they? Would it be true—as many would argue—that women, more than men, are preoccupied with personal relationships?

WILLIAMS I'm not sure that that is so. I am very interested by the extent to which, particularly younger generation people, male as well as female, put a far greater emphasis on personal relations, on personal self-discovery, on the arts, on their relations to their friends, than earlier generations did. There are worries about this; some of the Victorian sense of the duty one owes the community is beginning to disappear into a much greater absorption with the fulfilment of *myself*—though not entirely selfishly. I think some of it is an emphasis on the personal and private because the public and the community problems are so great and it is difficult to see solutions. The only thing I fear is that this increasing absorption in personal relationships—in many ways an excellent thing—could mean that we are not able to call on sufficient compassion and sympathy in the next generation for the collective concerns of the community. I think we have got to get the balance right.

MCCULLOCH Now surely, in the twentieth century, the distinction between the public and private is not so sharply drawn as it was in the nineteenth? I mean by that, that the family was always left absolutely free from all outside control—now, this is not so. The family is being invaded by all manner of outside controls, inevitably, and I would have thought that women would have emerged far more because of that.

WILLIAMS Well, I think the real reason why they have not is, as I have said, the pattern of the way in which our affairs are conducted. There are lots of things which are of immediate and great interest to women, whether one looks at such matters as equal pay or further legislation on the adoption and fostering of children, and one would like to see a few more women on the committees for such Bills. It isn't the substance of the matter of politics that prevents this; it is the fact that our institutions have not changed enough.

If I may make one rather boring generalization—but I think it is a crucial one—the problem with Britain and, to some extent with the whole of the democratic world, is that many of our institutions have not yielded enough to two major changes in our society—one is certainly the emergence of women, and, for that matter, the parallel emergence of people of different coloured skins—but secondly, our institutions have not changed sufficiently to reflect the much greater desire of people to participate in decisions. Whether one looks at the structure of industry or politics, what one sees are surging movements, surging pressures and new groups emerging. Meanwhile the institutions have not altered very much from the pattern of thirty or forty years ago; they have changed far less than the world around them.

McCulloch Now this lack of change is often blamed upon the solid mass of womankind who are reputed to be extremely slow to change. Do you think this is still true?

Williams I think women are very security-minded. They are more frightened of change for the very good biological reason that they protect their families against unknown factors coming from outside, whether it be disease or uncertainty or circumstance. And so, in all countries, women tend to be more conservative as voters—conservative with a small 'c' by the way! And I think that what we have to persuade women of is, that if you don't change certain institutions, you may create a much more explosive and dangerous situation than if you do. Can I give you an illustration?

I have long believed that the major changes in our education system—which mean that far more people now enjoy some sense of being able to express their views, question orthodox views—is an explosive mixture if poured into an industrial structure which is still purely authoritarian, where the Board makes its decision and the shop-floor accepts it. I do not believe you can run a liberal education system in which people are taught, up to the age of sixteen, to talk, question, discuss, and then expect them, when they start work at sixteen, to revert to behaving as they would have done in their nursery schools. It is this which is dangerous and that, in my view, leads to a great deal of industrial alienation in our country.

McCulloch Would you say that the wastage of first-class ability is one of the great tragedies of this century; the fact that so many really first-class women, for instance, are in third-rate jobs?

Williams It is a mystery to me. All my life I have been in school-rooms, lecture-rooms, university halls, jobs, with women more intelligent than myself. About their ability I have not the slightest doubt—it was considerably greater than mine in a number of cases—and I ask myself why should I, today, be a Cabinet Minister and they be, perhaps, working as a supply-teacher or a publisher's reader or something of that kind. And the reason is that, I think, women are easily discouraged.

If I wanted to put my finger on the problem about girls—or more precisely, perhaps, about their parents—it is a lack of aspiration for their daughters, a feeling that they ought to settle for less than those daughters are capable of, which people far more rarely feel about their sons. And although I don't believe that ambition is a great good—I don't think it necessarily leads to people having happy or, for that matter, well-balanced lives—what I am quite sure you should *not* do is to leave someone with a talent that can in no way be realized, because that can lead to great bitterness afterwards. It is the psychology of lack of confidence, I think, much more than lack of native ability, that has tended to undermine women's roles in our society.

McCulloch I agree. Now, when we had James Laver here he announced, very firmly, from that pulpit, that the patriarchal society was gone. This was just before the election and that was why I naturally expected, if he was right, that there would be more women M.P.s than ever before. In view of what you have just said, do you think he is wrong and that the patriarchal society is still with us?

Williams As far as the election went, I don't think there is any prejudice at all among voters any more. You run into the occasional elderly gentleman who makes some remark to the effect that nobody who wears skirts can think. I find among women, among younger men, there really is very little remaining prejudice, and almost all the evidence bears this out. Where a woman stands in a constituency she does no better and no worse than a man does. But I think that where it goes wrong is simply that women tend to get the tough seats. Now, if they start like men, let us say at the age of twenty-five, they fight a hopeless seat. But at the very point at which the man is moving on to a hopeful seat at the age of thirty-two or so, the woman, if she is married, is producing her first or second baby. It is as simple as that. When she comes back, if she is very keen, at the age of forty, all the seats are gone and she is beginning to look a bit old to fight her first marginal seat.

It is the problem of these ten or fifteen years in the middle that I was thinking about when I said that our society hasn't made changes for women. I'll give you one radical illustration of this. We still think in terms of higher education being something that you take between the ages of eighteen and twenty-one, which means that our women university graduates, our women doctors, architects and so on, move out, fully qualified into the professional world approximately two years before they are likely to produce their first baby. They are then out of the profession, not having ever really started in it. Ten or fifteen years later they come back and all that they have learnt is now rusted.

I would very much like to see a straight option for women, to offer them the chance of taking the higher education years—to which they are entitled if they get a university place—in, say, one year followed, ten years later, by another two years, or vice versa. I would like to see the possibility of it being done part-time, and of short residential courses to which children could be taken. Our structures all assume that women are men, that the pattern of their lives is the same as for men, and they then say, 'We have given you equality because we treat you the same'. We will never know what women can achieve until we change the pattern of our institutions to enable them to achieve it without having to sacrifice the years of raising their young children.

McCULLOCH Well, there is still a strange time-lag, which means that people see woman as, somehow, not rightly placed if she is in a position of management, although the whole of woman's training, as a rule, fits her far more than most men, for that very job.

WILLIAMS Let me bring it closer home. I am in some ways, I suppose, a bit conservative, so I find the idea of my standing there with your dog-collar on, a very odd one. But the Church is an institution which gives a lead, not least a moral lead, and yet the Church has—all the Churches have—virtually excluded women from any senior position at all. They are essentially seen as ancillaries, much more so, by the way, than they were in the thirteenth or fourteenth centuries. But the brief medieval period in which women did exercise this great influence in the Church, simply ceased to be. There is no woman bishop and it is inconceivable to most of us here, that there ever will be, at least as far ahead as we can see.

McCULLOCH Oh, Shirley, there flashed into my mind the wild hope that instead of being the first woman Prime Minister of this country. . . .

WILLIAMS No thank you!

McCULLOCH . . . you would be the first woman Archbishop of Canterbury! Because I think it might do us all a lot of good! I don't suppose you will consider it?

WILLIAMS I am afraid that you will have to assume total ecumenism if I do!

McCULLOCH Well, I will assume that at once. I certainly hope though, seriously, that before very long we will, in the Church, take certain definite steps towards reform in this matter. Because as things now stand, exactly half the human race is denied equal opportunity to be of some value in this particular way to the rest of mankind.

But do you see, in this half of the twentieth century, any clear creative movement forward? Is there any new thought emerging—in the field of politics, say?

WILLIAMS I am quite glad you have left women for a bit, because I tend to find I spend more time than I sometimes want to, talking about this one aspect, and I should say for myself, that I really see the position of women as a part of the position of being underprivileged and not as special to itself.

Yes, I think that we are moving into an era of new politics, and I don't mean just party politics here. It has got many aspects to it, ranging from the whole question of how we draw budgets that save resources rather than use them; the technology of saving energy and raw materials; of really taking the message the environmentalists have been giving us. The talk about planet Earth is the talk about tomorrow and not about the next century any more.

Then there are aspects in the new politics concerning the whole field of participation. This is terribly difficult, because people want far more participation than they have had in the past, but they also want rapid decisions, and the two often conflict. So we must get the balance right. I think the answer here must lie in the devolution of power, down and down to the lowest possible groups, like neighbourhood groups, that can exercise power.

I think, thirdly, that we are in a period when our relations with the outside world need very careful looking at, because there is one danger I see, and it arises in all our political parties—also among the general public—and that is a tendency to become rather markedly insular, to turn our backs upon the problems of the world and say, 'Good God, with so many problems of our own to solve, we can't possibly do anything about *that*!' This would, in my view, be terribly dangerous and we could rapidly enter into a kind of beggar-my-neighbour situation over all the raw materials and so on, which, in the end, would serve nobody.

Finally, I want to say that I think we can pick upon that point I mentioned earlier: the interest of the younger generation in what one might describe as the more personal and private aspects of life, so that politics can be enriched by a greater interest in the arts, in education—continuing life-long education rather than formal education—in the whole pursuit of knowledge by all of us in ways we haven't yet explored. I'm sorry if that is a bit vague, but when one is on the edge of a major revolution it is difficult to chart the way. I use the word 'revolution', not as the simple, old-fashioned term that Marx used, but as a much more fascinating one that goes much deeper and has many more spiritual as well as economic elements in it. I am sure that the way ahead is going to be strange and exciting, and probably frightening and quite new.

12 March 1974

Oxford knew him best most of his life as a familiar and much loved don. The undergraduates would see him in the High, and identify him with a certain pride. 'There goes the Goldsmith's Professor of English Literature.' Or a fellow-don would sight him. 'That was David Cecil.' (He always walks fast, as though anxious to avoid the discourtesy of being late.) He was the very reverse of Belloc's 'remote and ineffectual Don'. In fact, he was an ideal don, happily at home alike with the undergraduates as with his fellow senior members. His conversation, lectures, writings always opened windows, and enhanced the pleasures of the mind. And as Oxford most appreciates a distinctive and rare personality, there was a certain proprietorial delight in its regard for him. Above all, he had the unfailing knack of sharing his enjoyment and interest in living with all and sundry.

Now he is in retirement at Cranborne. At times, he emerges to make a public appearance, and on two occasions it has been our good fortune to hear him in dialogue at St Mary-le-Bow—both singularly memorable because he communicated to City workers the same enhanced sense of life's being well worth living which he had given to many in the kindlier climate of Oxford.

He talks with immense rapidity. Before his second visit, his wife, who was RADA trained, warned him that he must try to speak much more slowly and deliberately. Despite the fact that it is not really in his nature to orate, he did achieve a considerable decrease in the speed of his utterance (about twice the pace, therefore, of most speakers). Not a word was missed, nor yet one of the sudden chuckles with which he punctuates his discourse.

His writing, however, betrays no hint of haste. There is no more beautiful prose than his in contemporary literature. *The Stricken Deer* and *Two Quiet Lives* and his biography of Melbourne are three of the literary treasures of an age noted for the making of many books but few of great quality.

DIALOGUE WITH

David Cecil

McCulloch Lord David Cecil's life has been in many fields, but mainly in what is called Literature, to which he has done great service. I am puzzled by this word *literature*; it is such a vague word, in some ways. I picked up a thing called *The Bible Designed to be Read as Literature*, and I was reading it before you came. What on earth did they mean by that title?

Cecil I think what they meant was that the Bible could be read and enjoyed even if one didn't believe in it. Here is this famous great work which has generally been read as the word of God! Well, many people, in the view of the editor, no longer took it to be the word of God but thought it was a very splendid piece of writing. So he said, 'Don't bother about whether you believe it or not; read it as you would, the works of Shakespeare or Milton, for its literary value'.

McCulloch But is literature, therefore, any written thing, or is it more precisely to be defined?

Cecil Like a great many words, it is used in different senses and one understands it according to the context. It can just mean anything printed or written. Supposing, for instance, you were going abroad and you went to the travel agents and said, 'I want to go to the South', he might say, 'Well, there is a lot of literature about that over there'. He would mean that there was a lot of written stuff that you could read up about it. But if I said, at Oxford—I am retired now but I used to teach there—'I teach English literature', I didn't mean I just taught English written stuff; I meant that I taught the English books which are also works of art.

McCulloch But has literature the same power of outlasting other works of art as, say, great architecture or great painting?

Cecil That depends. It has got one advantage: you can have copies of books, and if one is destroyed, well then, there are the others left. There are many copies of Shakespeare, but if St Paul's Cathedral were destroyed, there aren't replicas of it that you could look at instead.

McCulloch May I just go off the point for the moment and ask, would you collect First Editions?

Cecil No I wouldn't, but I don't think other people shouldn't. Everybody has a right to his own taste. I have never been a bibliophile, but a lot of people I like and respect very much, are. It is a taste, like a taste for croquet.

McCulloch Because I was thinking that when I was at Warwick, we discovered in the church library there a unique Caxton. It was a very ugly piece of printing, an early Caxton that people knew existed—I believe the Fitzwilliam had a few pages—but we actually found the book, the only copy extant, and of course, there was great excitement about it. I took a very iconoclastic view and said, 'Well, what nonsense! It is only a few bits of the Bible and you can get the whole thing for a few shillings, and better printed, too.' And they wanted to give us £25,000 for this. It seemed to me ironical.

Cecil Well, if you can get £25,000 for something, I think it is very pleasant. But this interest in old books is a special kind of interest and a perfectly worthy one, though it isn't the same as an interest in literature, any more than an interest in old stones and geology is an interest in architecture.

McCulloch I agree! Now, about 100 years ago, say, the Bible would be *the* literature, of this country, really, would it not?

Cecil The Bible in those days was the book which anybody who could read, had most likely read something of; and therefore it had a unique position. Even if there was no other book in a house, there was likely to be a Bible; and its language, its allusions and stories, had got, as it were, into the language. People could mention them and it was known what they were talking about; so it gave a centre to the culture of England.

McCulloch The curious thing is that the Bible became discredited because it hadn't got the facts right. You know, it said certain things about the origin of man and so on, and it was all wrong apparently. The Church had an argument about the Bible which went on for fifty years, and by that time it had become discredited. Most people were very disillusioned.

Cecil Wouldn't it be fairer to say that some of it was discredited? For instance, the story of Adam and Eve came to be taken much more as a myth, and in a sense *that* was discredited. But I have never heard anybody say that they thought less of the Gospel of St John.

McCulloch Curiously enough, I think they did. I think the whole Bible became discredited.

Cecil That was very inconsequent of them.

McCulloch Well, it is a fact that very few people read it now. Many of your predecessors in that pulpit, who are very distinguished people like yourself, show a surprising lack of knowledge of the Bible or what is in it. Perhaps not quite so bad as the brilliant Greek scholar—you must have heard this story—who was being viva'd at Oxford by, I presume, some of your colleagues. They gave him a bit of the crucifixion story to read, and he wouldn't stop although they said, 'Thank you, that will do' and, 'Thank you. Stop please!' but he went on and on and at last he looked up and said, 'I'm so sorry! I just wanted to see how it ended.' An old story; I'm sorry!

Lord David, is it not a fact that a nation, or a civilization, is very much held together by its literature?

Cecil I wonder about 'held together'. Yet, in a sense, literature *does* embody in words the nation, because it is in one language. You can talk about English literature and this doesn't merely mean a lot of books that happen to be written in one country—England. It means books that have something in common because they use special words and grammar to say what they mean, which aren't the same words and grammar as another country uses, and there aren't equivalents. Anybody who has tried to translate will find this out, because the words and the way words are used, are really the expression of the way that people think. So you see, the language does express the whole mode of thought and feeling and imagination of a nation, of a people.

McCulloch It is a fact, of course, that the world is now brought together, in a sense, by the curious accident of English becoming the common language, is it not?

Cecil Yes, originally, I suppose, because of the great spread by the English people across the United States, now the dominating power. But also there is Canada, Australia, New Zealand; all over the world, where the English have been, the language has spread. But of course, the language begins to alter. I would say that the way the Americans use the language isn't the same as our way. They use it very well, but in a way growingly different from the way we use it. I don't just mean their slang and colloquial expressions. The different immigrant groups in America—the middle Europeans and particularly the Germans

—have imported modes of thought which have begun to alter the way in which one expresses oneself.

McCulloch May I take up this phrase, 'mode of thinking', because the mode of thinking in this country has certainly changed tremendously in the last 100 years or so. We used to be traditional in the way we thought, but nowadays we are rationalistic. Do you think that the disappearance of the Bible as the sort of cement of thought, would be the main factor in that change?

Cecil It certainly would be a big factor. But, you know, I would a little question that the tradition has altered as much as all that. Obviously, the whole world in the last 100 years, has seen the biggest changes since the—whenever it was—perhaps the Bronze Age, and that has made an incredible difference to the way that people think and look at things. But their moral concepts, their ideas of, say, a good man, an attractive woman, haven't altered all that much; and they are very English still. I am interested always, when I am looking at the plays of Shakespeare, which, I suppose, are the nearest thing we have to a sacred book, to note how different some of his concepts and ideals are from what you find in foreign literature, and how much they are still true of England. Take two examples: his ideal of the heroine; there are two sorts in Shakespeare, there is the gentle, affectionate, submissive kind like Desdemona, and there is the resourceful, lively, spirited kind like Rosalind and Beatrice and Portia. These two types persist; you can trace them right down through English literature. If you read the great Russian or French novels, they contain nobody like either of them. It is an English ideal. Or again, the idea of a good king. Henry V is Shakespeare's hero-king, and he is heroic and commanding and royal, but he is also democratic and genial, and hobnobs with the soldiers. No doubt that was the ideal represented by Queen Elizabeth I; it is utterly unlike anything you read about Louis XIV and the Czars of Russia. It is an English ideal. I think it is still what people look for in a King of England, or a member of the Royal Family. These traditions go on.

McCulloch Would it be true also of humour? Could you trace, for instance, the same tradition of English humour in our literature, say, from Shakespeare to Jane Austen?

Cecil Good Lord, yes! You can go back to Chaucer and the Canterbury Tales and find what we call the English type of humour, it comes down through Shakespeare and—oh yes—

right through Fielding, Dickens and also the more delicate humour of Jane Austen; they are all of a kind. Yes, I think humour is very typical.

There are two authors I am particularly fond of and put very high: Jane Austen and Thomas Hardy. I have never got a foreign person to agree with me about either of them. They admire Dickens—and Shakespeare, no doubt; but these other two writers, no. I think it is because, in their different ways, Hardy and Jane Austen are so profoundly English that one has to be English to appreciate the strength and subtleties of their writing.

McCulloch Yes, indeed. But do you think it is sad that a nation should lose a sacred literature? That is to say, a literature it regards as authoritative?

Cecil I think it is a pity to lose the Bible, because I am a Christian and I think it is true. If other people don't feel that it is, then they are losing a lot.

McCulloch But we are in a situation at the moment where more than half the world has accepted a kind of sacred literature in Karl Marx.

Cecil That is a terrible state to have got into. It is quite unreadable apart from anything else; and mostly untrue.

McCulloch I certainly can't read it! But I just think that here we are, in Western civilization, or whatever it is called, but we haven't got any equivalent, have we?

Cecil Well, as I say, we are lucky not to have *that*. I suppose it is a pity that we haven't got something to focus on; but I don't know, we have got a lot of splendid things to read and they have enough in common for us to make our own individual sacred books. I don't feel it matters very much, honestly.

McCulloch Curiously enough, people seem to be reading more these days, despite what they say about us being transfixed by the gogglebox. I asked the City Librarian before you came, and he told me that it is quite an incredible figure at the Cannon Street Library, for instance, something like 800,000 issues every year, which is a great deal. Is it a more literate world, do you think?

Cecil Well, I feel a little hesitant because I have never studied this question, and when you get to my age one often generalizes about younger people, and is wrong; so I hesitate here. I think it is true, judging by the young people I have had to deal with. Certainly they don't read as much as people, similar to themselves, would have done forty years ago, but this is for the reasons you give, that there are other alternatives, such as television and the cinema and other activities. It is a gain and a loss. It is a pity that they don't get all the fun out of reading that I did. But if all these books as you say, are taken out of the library, it is most likely that reading is still a very widespread habit.

McCulloch Writing books and reading them are presumably methods of communicating. But the cynic—or he may be the realist—says that although more books pour out from the publishers today, yet ironically enough, there is even less to be said.

Cecil Oh Dear! I would have to read much more of what is being written before I would know that there was very little to be said. It may be that here are new things to be said and people haven't yet found the way to say them. I think this does happen. You see, gradually, forms were invented, the poetic play and the novel and so on. A form was always invented for a purpose, in order to say something in the best possible way. Then what happens is, that the world changes. But the form doesn't so people try to twist the form, and adapt it, to suit the new subject matter, the new point of view. Generally, as these literary forms are pretty flexible, they can be adapted. But I do think, with the very big changes that there have been recently, it is harder to adapt to the old forms than it was in the past. I say this questioningly because I have not thought about it very much. I may be wrong. But I feel that this is the difficulty. Possibly television and films do say some of these new things more easily than a book does.

McCulloch I have a sort of persistent and obstinate idea that a book is a better way, in the long run, of saying them.

Cecil Well, I think it is better for saying a lot of things because you have more space and more leisure. After all, a television programme may have to take only forty or fifty minutes. You cannot get a lot into that. That is one problem. The other thing is, when you write a book, you do have an idea of the kind of person you hope is going to read it. That is much easier, I think, than writing for television, because there you don't know who is going to turn the television set on.

McCulloch I think this is very true. I have a feeling that long after the television has been forgotten they will be turning over the pages of your books!

CECIL I don't know about *my* books, but I certainly think they will turn over the pages of some books. That is partly, of course, because a book is easier to keep than a television film.

McCULLOCH One thing the City Librarian said that interested me was that the most popular form of reading at the moment—I think, Lord David, you will be rather glad about this—is biography. Why is that?

CECIL I am delighted. It is the kind of book that I write! I can only suggest a reason. I think it is that we live in a scientific age and the great things that it will be remembered for, will inevitably be, I think, great scientific discoveries. This means that people are very much more conditioned to be interested in facts, and things that can be factually proved, than in fanciful forms of art. Now a biography, if it is a good biography, is a work of literature; it shows imagination and a sense of style and all that. But also it records facts. If you are a conscientious biographer, you do check your facts and keep true to them. So I think that is one reason that people like biographies.

The other reason is, I think, that people have become very interested in psychology and in human beings, how they relate themselves to society, how character is conditioned and how it functions. These interests, of course, are well provided for by a biography. It will tell you about a man's family and the influences on his childhood and how these, combined with his own innate nature, make him the kind of person he is. Then, of course, he has to be related to the world outside, and how the relations between them produces the story of his life.

McCULLOCH Isn't the main continuing theme of all great literature the aspiration of man to a kind of nobility?

CECIL Yes. We live in an imperfect world, full of glory and beauty, but also flawed, full of disappointment and imperfection. But, because we are born with something in us that desires the perfect, we are always searching for it. What a good book does, is to give you the picture of something in real life but transformed by imagination and the skill of the writer, into something else that *does* seem like an image of perfection. This is what makes you delight in art and music and pictures. It is like life and true to life; but it is better than life.

McCULLOCH May I just add a footnote to that question? Most people at the moment are feeling that what they look for in modern literature is not there, namely, some vision of life which lifts man out of the rather day to day grimness.

CECIL That is true; but I think they will get it, if the author has this vision. He may describe something prosaic and humdrum and even with some horror in it; but if he himself has the sensibility and the feeling of what is good and beautiful, this will appear both in the way he tells his story, and in the incidents or people that he talks about. There will always be the sign of some higher, more desirable form of life there, even if he shows it, as it were, only by its absence.

9 September 1967

An obviously envious wit defined the specialist as one who knew more and more about less and less—a narrowing process which James Laver, an outstanding example of those who make a field of knowledge unchallengeably their own, has constantly avoided. While it is undeniably true that his greatest fame has been as one of our foremost authorities on the history of costume, a glance at his published works and studies will at once reveal the astonishing breadth and versatility of his talents. I have long been among those who regarded him with something of the awe Goldsmith described:

> And still they gazed, and still the wonder grew
> That one small head could carry all he knew.

While keeper of various departments at the Victoria and Albert Museum, he turned his hand to sundry arts outside his special field, writing, poetry, drama, biography, a musical comedy libretto, critical essays, a children's play, short stories—time would fail me to enumerate them all. In fact, he seems to have lived several lives at once, and although now in his seventies, and physically rather frail, the inspiration and zest which have always made him unusually alive still charge him with the vigour of a human dynamo. As a communicator of words and ideas James Laver is electrifying.

Although a historian, he is by no means immersed in the past. The modern scene fascinates him. He enjoys being alive in an age of radical change and social revolution. He is very much a prophet, in the sense that he sees the shape of the future adumbrated in the world of today. As he reads the signs of our times, his vision of the future is, for a man of his years, full of a curiously youthful hope for the world which will be after him, and indeed after most of us who were listening to him. Our lunch-hour with James Laver left us invigorated, pondering, and, as usual, like the Great Bell of Bow, still not knowing.

DIALOGUE WITH

James Laver

McCulloch I have for many years had a great admiration for James Laver, whose influence on the ideas of both the theatre and art in general, has been tremendous. He is, without doubt, the greatest authority—certainly in this country—on the history of what we wear, and I want to draw him out on the whole significance of costume.

Now, Mr Laver, you have defined the reasons why we put on clothes and the way we put them on as first, utility; secondly, the conferring of status or the expression of status; and thirdly, the whole business of attracting each other sexually. Where at the moment do you think we are in these three things?

Laver On the edge of a revolution more important than any that has happened in the last three thousand years, because we are witnessing the end of the patriarchal system. Almost the whole of recorded history has been written within the period of the patriarchal system, and we tend to think therefore that patriarchalism has lasted forever. But for thousands of years *before* the patriarchal system was established, there was matriarchy. A woman's family consisted of her children and her brothers, and the father of the children was an intruder from another tribe, and not always the same man. So that no one in the primitive community knew who his father was. It would have been no good saying, 'It's a wise child that knows his own father', because nobody did know, no matter how wise he was. And this was the normal condition of society. And aren't we fast getting back to that condition today?

Last time I was in America, I heard the American version of the story of the Three Bears: 'Once upon a time there were three bears; there was Father Bear, Mother Bear, and Baby Bear by a previous marriage.' Well—maybe we haven't got that far in this country yet, but by God, we are going that way! You go and stay with people, and there is a charming hostess and three lively children, and the man who fixes you a drink. And go three years later and it's all the same, except for the man who fixes you a drink, who is someone quite different! That is the situation. And if it is so, then we are on the eve of a real revolution in social history. You see, female emancipation is incompatible with the patriarchal system, which consisted, as all human institutions do, in a sanction: 'Leave my house, faithless woman!' If all you can say is, 'I will now leave your house, faithless woman', the game is up. Man is dwindled to a function.

What we are entering now is a period of female supremacy. You see, you can plot the degree of male domination at any moment, by considering the height of the hat. This may sound quite absurd but I think it is true. The last peak of male domination was 1850, shall we say? And if you look at the fashion-plates of the time, you'll find that they all wore top-hats. Then in 1880 the New Woman made her appearance and all the men went into gents' boaters. I don't want to overdo the Freudian implications, but putting on a hat, according to Freud, is a gesture of virility, and the higher your hat, the more dominant you are in that field. Well, gents' boaters in 1880 were much less high than top-hats in 1850, and in this present century, when women had really won the game, both sexes gave up wearing hats altogether. You can see it for yourself, can't you? When I travel in a tube train, I look around me and I see that nobody is wearing a hat.

McCULLOCH But in your admirable book, which has become a classic, *The History of Costume*, you say that there are three reasons why we clothe ourselves. We started because—you call it 'utility', I believe—because we needed to keep warm, and to protect our nakedness in one way or another. Then you say, we went on to develop our clothes to demonstrate to what social class we belonged and thirdly, we put on clothes in order to—especially the female—demonstrate our attractiveness to the other sex.

LAVER I would stick to that. I think that the three principles of costume are first, the utility principle which is very unimportant. There are people who live in what I believe is called, Tierra del Fuego. And they haven't got round to the idea of clothing at all. They simply have a piece of skin which they hang round their necks and shift according to the prevailing wind. And it's a very cold climate!

I agree that there are these three principles: there is the seduction principle, dressing to attract the opposite sex; there is the hierarchical principle, dressing to demonstrate your social class; and there is the utility principle, which has hardly any influence at all. You see, the utility principle prevents women from wearing clothes which are sixty yards in circumference, but not from wearing clothes which are six yards in circumference, which they did in the 1860s. It prevents men from wearing clothes where they can't breathe at all, but not from wearing clothes in which they can only just breathe, which I am doing at the moment. The utility principle is a very poor third.

Of course, for the greater part of the history of male costume, clothes were deliberately designed to make it impossible to work. Certainly, they are less formal now than they were. In my early days at the Victoria and Albert Museum, when we heard that Queen Mary was coming to see the Museum, we used to take a taxi home, and put on a morning coat. And when they opened the present Victoria and Albert Museum, all the senior officials hired full court dress, with swords! Incredible, isn't it?

McCULLOCH Yes. I think I prefer my cassock. That's the easiest thing in the world to wear, because it is like a dressing gown!

Originally, I suppose, there were only two kinds of clothes, roughly speaking: the bifurcated and the frock type?

LAVER Yes, but the rules are not absolute, because, you see, the Chinese women have always worn trousers and Persian women have always worn trousers.

McCULLOCH I didn't think it had necessarily anything to do with sex, but there are just these two kinds of dress, aren't there?

LAVER Yes. What the anthropologists call tropical clothing and Arctic clothing. Arctic clothes are trousers and tropical clothes are skirts. After all, the Romans wore skirts, or kilts, and it was considered a barbarism when Roman soldiers began to wear trousers.

McCULLOCH But there was no question, in the early stages of mankind, of differentiating the sexes by clothes, was there?

LAVER No. That, of course, was the great triumph of patriarchalism. From the Bible days onwards, it was very important to make it quite clear who was male and who was female. Well, it has all gone by the board. I walk behind people in Blackheath, where I live, and they've both got long hair, they are both wearing jeans, and you have to go round to the side to see which is the woman and which the man.

McCULLOCH It doesn't always work that way either! I agree, but what is the significance of this, socially? Now, I am going to quote you. 'In the perspective of costume history', you have written, 'it is plain that the dress of any given period is exactly suited to the social climate of the time.'

LAVER Well, nothing could be more different in 1850 than the clothes of a man and the clothes of a woman. A woman was wearing a crinoline, a man was wearing a frock-coat and a top-hat. But that is not so any longer, and that is due to the emancipation of women. There have been waves of female emancipation in the past, the one we've already spoken of, in 1880, for instance, when all the men went into gents' boaters. And in 1800 they were more emancipated than in 1840, but now the wave of female emancipation has gone over the seawall and there is no going back. All very well, I approve of it in many ways but, as some housewife said to me rather sadly the other day, 'The net result of female emancipation is that I am always washing up!'

MCCULLOCH I can't help feeling that that housewife is unusual, because *I* seem to be always washing up too! But you think, in fact, female emancipation in this particular society has come to stay and we are looking forward to a situation where man and woman will confront each other on equal terms?

LAVER Yes, if that is ever possible, given the disabilities of women. But it seems to be the way we are going and certainly it means a revolution in costume. Because you see, young men today are saying—don't look at old fuddy-duddies like me—'I repudiate the tradition of gentility'. The thing that Beau Brummel managed to get established was that there is no difference among gentlemen. Even if one of them is called George Brummel and one is called George, Prince of Wales. We are all on the same level and our top-hats are all on the same level. On this exalted plateau, all gentlemen are equal. At the same time, while feeling equal among their peers, they felt superior to those of a lower social order and superior towards the female of the species. But all this has gone to the winds now. The young men who buy their clothes in Carnaby Street would be insulted if you suggested they looked like gentlemen, wouldn't they?

MCCULLOCH Well, it would be untrue. But what about the women? What are they rebelling against?

LAVER According to Professor Fluegel, the dominating factor in women's clothes is what he calls the 'shifting erogenous zone'. And if that sounds too psychological for you, what it means is this: that the body of a woman is a seductive object, and the mind of man is too weak to take it all in at once. So he has to concentrate on one particular bit of it, and it is the function of fashion to keep shifting this bit around to freshen the palate, so to speak. This is known as the 'shifting erogenous zone'.

McCULLOCH Would not that lead any student of costume—as you are and no one so good—to suggest that we are all bats? Because, quite clearly, there is no rationality in all this, is there?

LAVER No, clothes are quite irrational. Fashion is an outrage. It was only invented in the fourteenth century; for a thousand years before that, clothes hadn't altered at all. Women wore the same clothes as they had worn at the fall of the Roman Empire. And then, suddenly, in the Courts of France and Burgundy, fashion began: the idea that it was natural for women's clothes to change rapidly. It may sound an unreasonable boast but I can date brass-rubbings in the late fourteenth century, by the hair-do, to within a couple of years. This was an absolutely new idea.

And of course, for the greater part of history, servants' clothes—if I may use the term—were twenty years behind the times. You see, when you walked in the streets—and this was true even in my childhood—you knew a woman's social class by the clothes she was wearing. You don't know now, because owing to the fashion magazines and the modern media, they can be reproduced anywhere, any time you like, and so the only advantage a rich woman has over her poorer sister is a fortnight's start.

McCULLOCH It is most interesting, this, because it reveals my enormous Achilles' heel. For the life of me, I have not noticed for donkey's years, how a woman was dressed. And this I have to confess. I honestly can't look back and tell you what my wife was wearing ten, twenty, even *five* years ago! Surely this art of seduction, if it is going to be expressed in clothes, has got to reckon with the fact that enormous numbers of men are unobservant?

LAVER But when a man says: 'Oh, don't bother to do this, that or the other, my dear wife, just come for a walk with me in the clothes you were wearing last month', she will know perfectly well, if she is a clever woman, that this won't do. She will know, because she has watched his eyes, as they pass other women in the street, how they swivel round.

McCULLOCH Yes, I see what you mean. Now that leads me on to what I was trying to say, that I think women's fashion has significance only for other women.

LAVER Well, I have invented a formula. Any woman will tell you that she dresses to please herself. 'I express my own personality' she says. But isn't it curious that she expresses her own personality by dressing in exactly the fashion of the day? It operates on the level of the collective unconscious. Fashion is outside the control of the conscious mind altogether. Take the great fashion designers of the Twenties—Worth, Paquin, Patou, Schiaparelli—most of whom I knew. *There* are people who lived by being original, and yet if you look at the drawings or photographs of their costumes, there is no difference. You can't say, Patou, Schiaparelli, Worth, Paquin. All you can say is 1925, 1926, 1927 and so on. They were all doing the same thing. Now this means that the thing is outside the control of the conscious mind altogether.

McCulloch My wife tells me—I don't know whether she's right or not—that, in fact, the real fashion today for women is to be free of fashion; that is to say, to dress how you like, to turn out in your grandmother's clothes if you want to.

Laver Yes, there is a degree of fantasy. You see, women have only three choices: they can be in the fashion, they can be dowdy, or they can be in fancy-dress. They are the only three choices they have. And today, a lot of them are choosing fancy-dress. And of course, the fashion houses now are bust, the whole lot of them. They live by selling perfume. The people who go and watch the fashion shows in Paris are just wasting their time.

In 1946, I brought out a little book called: *A Letter to a Girl on the Future of Clothes*, and, basing myself entirely on historical analogies, I said, 'In ten years' time, women will have very plain dresses with the waist in the wrong place, as in 1800, after the French Revolution, when it was very high, or in 1924, after the First World War, when it was very low'. And this was received with the utmost hostility—not even hostility—the utmost scepticism, by the fashion commentators, who said, 'Whatever does this man in a museum know about it? We go over to Paris twice a year . . .' and all that. And it was an unfortunate moment for me because Dior had just brought out his New Look which was the exact opposite of what I was saying. Ten years later, however, Dior was so obliging as to bring out first the A-look and then the H-look, and women were back in the Twenties as I had said they would be. Since then my stock with the rag-trade has been rather high.

McCulloch I should think so! Well, now we seem to be moving into an age which as your shrewd eye will see, is quite different from any other. Apart from anything else, surely there is going to be a greater degree of equality between the sexes, is there not? The patriarchal system has gone, and we are not expecting a return of the matriarchal system, are we?

LAVER I'm not sure. Anyway, patriarchy is finished, and the function of the father is shrinking into insignificance. I've told you the story of the Three Bears; that is where we are going.

McCULLOCH But it may be very different from what we now fear or think. I mean that there may suddenly arrive a new wave of sanity. Suppose there were to emerge between the sexes, a sudden recognition that this adversativeness was all wrong, and a realization of what they really were to each other. Is this beyond belief?

LAVER I'm not sure that you are not asking for the return of Hitler, because his motto was, 'Kirche, Kinde, Küche'. In other words, women get back to the children, the Church and the kitchen! But that is not going to happen.

McCULLOCH No, I wasn't thinking of that. I was wondering whether a quite new relationship might not arrive, emerging through all this curious mess-up and confusion of our times. Isn't it possible that a kind of comradeship which I already see between young people of different sexes, might become the norm?

LAVER Yes, I think it might. But that doesn't mean sticking to one man.

McCULLOCH Curiously enough, the females that I know, *want* to stick to one man. The difficulty at the moment is keeping the young man to stick to *them*—which I think is really the problem. Because young men today are obviously disorientated and confused.

LAVER Most normal young men want to have a family, but one has to face the fact that while women, generally speaking, are monogamous, men are *not* monogamous. I have more faith in women than I have in men, I must say.

22 January 1974

Jacquetta Hawkes admirably combines the distinctive attributes of womanhood with a no less distinctive ability of mind and scholarship. Two of her books, *A Land* and *Man on Earth* bring to archeological study a poetic imagination which rarely distinguishes that field of knowledge.

A theme which frequently recurs in the dialogues is that of the position of women in society. It would seem that there are few live topics which can be discussed without the need to refer at some point to the fundamental change which is behind and within most of the social questions arising in the twentieth century, i.e. the emergence of woman as the equal of man in personal status. But the idea of the patriarchal society dies hard. There are still those—perhaps the majority—who can be surprised to find that an outstanding scholar is also a charming and attractive woman. That 'also' must often have amused Jacquetta Hawkes, and, I suspect, her husband J. B. Priestley, even more.

His field is the modern, whereas Jacquetta's is the ancient. But for both their common study and ruling interest is mankind itself. Many were surprised when the lovely Jacquetta Priestley joined in the Aldermaston marches in protest against the possession of nuclear weapons. Perhaps the most characteristic feature of her personality is a quality of rare reticence. She therefore surprised many by participating in a public demonstration. But those who really know her not only understood why she felt she ought thus to be visibly counted among the protesters, but also how far from easy it was for her to do this. It has never been enough for her merely to grace the groves of Academe. Precisely because she is a genuine woman, she is primarily a deeply feeling person. And there are times when one surprises oneself as well as others by the need to authenticate in action the expression of deep feeling. It is never enough merely to study mankind: there must be something one can do to show that it is well worth saving from itself.

DIALOGUE WITH

Jacquetta Hawkes

McCulloch I would like to talk about civilization, which was so interestingly deployed on television by Kenneth Clark. And you have very much distinguished yourself in understanding the civilizations of long ago.

Here we are, living in a technological age, and we have long since ceased to imagine what it would be like to live in the distant past—would it be as much fun, because we don't seem to be enjoying ourselves tremendously at the moment? Take the Bronze Age, for instance, would it have been as enjoyable a human life, do you think, in those days?

Hawkes Obviously one depends very much on one's own imagination, but then you *have* to grant that. I think that with the very first emergence of civilization in Sumeria and Egypt—about 5,000 years ago—you are catching the freshly created civilized man, a thing that can hardly happen again, because we have become constantly more self-conscious. You glimpse the whole range of human creativity coming straight out of the psyche of man, without any intellectual interference. But there is a danger, when thinking of the earliest civilized people, of putting too much emphasis on technology. One tends to assume that if you don't have, at least, a lavatory and perhaps something that will take you a lot faster than your own feet, or a certain number of gadgets in the house, then you must be in some way, a bit backward and defective, and moreover, that you must *miss* these things. And I think that is what the feat of the imagination must do, to make one see that if nobody had ever heard of a water-closet or a car, then they wouldn't feel the lack of them. I think the important thing to remember is that technology is not necessarily the same thing as civilization.

McCulloch The curious thing is that many people today are obviously trying to get away from technology, because they now take their children camping, which is really returning to the situation in which they were, probably, in the Bronze Age or even earlier.

HAWKES Yes, I think there has been a great coming-round to a pre-civilized thing, which is very interesting, because it shows that we have got these basic needs which demand to find satisfaction. I do think that a great many things would have been more enjoyable and indeed, more desirable, had one lived then. I suppose there were two big categories. The first one was that you were completely and directly involved in life and society at first hand. There was no theory of education; you went to school (if you were lucky enough to belong to the social classes that went to school); there was no theory of economics to worry about; you just saw that life required you to earn your living.

I often feel now, that I don't know how half the things that I depend on are organized and I wouldn't in the least know what to do if they broke down. They did not suffer from that at all; everything was more or less comprehensible to them, and everything was under their own control. They put up their houses, they cultivated their fields or their gardens, they produced their own food, and what they didn't produce they bought in the little market. They didn't have the feeling that we have, I think, that something from outside can completely ruin one and change one's life.

MCCULLOCH Are you saying, in fact, that the main distinction between our civilization and theirs would be something akin to a sense of security? Yet our civilization makes almost a god of security, doesn't it? Everywhere around you, particularly here in the City, are insurance companies. Do you think this is a sign of our basic *insecurity*?

HAWKES Yes, I think there is rather a paradox there, because in a way I think they did feel more secure, because of the fact that there were no great forces beyond their comprehension.

The second big category I was thinking of concerns something more important even than that. I feel sure, from all the religious literature which they have left—hymns and songs and accounts of festivals, and so on—that they did have a marvellous sense of relationship with God, or the gods, and with nature. Somehow they all felt they belonged to a society decreed by the gods and that their job was simply to serve them in the right way. And this attitude found expression in the great festivals and jollifications. The cycle of the year provided the framework into which the various festivities fitted, celebrating agricultural life, with the idea of fertility and spirits. They had a great sense of *shape*, and of the turning cycle of the seasons, of being young and sprouting up and dying. I believe that this sense of the completeness of society, and its relation with the year, with nature, with God, really was a fundamental superiority. And then the actual festivals were obviously tremendously jolly, particularly in Egypt where they had a great many parties. And you know, Joseph, all the girls were beautifully dressed in transparent shifts. And you get the point about the Women's Lib. idea: there was no need for bras there, you just had this beautiful little bosom showing through, fringed with lovely flowers that you put round your neck.

McCULLOCH But in fact you have not mentioned another important difference: that they didn't suffer from over-population.

HAWKES Of course, that is very true. I'm glad you reminded me of that, because I do think it must have been overwhelmingly important. You could easily get complete quiet and there wasn't a great deal of noise or rush at all.

McCULLOCH An enviable state! Our difficulty is that we have so plentifully peopled the earth that it has become very dangerous indeed. In those days, God apparently said, 'Be fruitful and multiply!' In these days, if God is heard at all, he is surely saying, 'For heaven's sake, stop it!'

HAWKES This links up, as it happens, with the first of my points *against*, which is the simple materialistic one that there was much sickness and no medicine, and that death was always among people. I think this must have been very terrible, that people were struck down all the time—it must have been a part of everyday life—and that there was so little you could do. But on the other hand, as you say, it did avoid the horror of over-population.

McCULLOCH This is our big problem now and technology is not offering any real solution. And this makes a difference in our lives, especially for women. And yet, in the days of the Bronze Age, women would be recognized as having a very important function—apart from child-bearing—wouldn't they?

HAWKES Oh yes, indeed they had. I have always thought it was a great support to women in all early societies that goddesses were so important, and rather before this Bronze Age civilization, the supreme deity undoubtedly *was* taken to be feminine. I can't doubt that that must have given women much more confidence in their own powers.

I would like to mention one or two other bad things, as one doesn't want to give a sentimentally glowing picture. I have spoken of ordinary sickness and death. There was also warfare, this dreadful thing which men seem to get involved in as soon as they can organize anything. I think Bronze Age warfare must have been absolutely ghastly, as it involved almost everybody. Of course, this is something which has continued down to our own times and one can't say that it is better now, or worse, but I think it probably afflicted them more immediately.

And then, we must give a little thought to the mind. I think it must have been a great loss to have had, not only no real sense of history, but no accumulation of treasures, of works of art and music and so on. You just had your own immediately accessible things. I do think that one should be grateful in our own times for the amazing treasure that we have inherited. And then, I suppose, another lack would have been intellectual interests—because in spite of the tremendous fullness of the religious life, for most people there was no really detached intellectual life. That didn't come until the time of the Greeks, so I think both these things were disadvantages. I think they had a number of rather simple games with which they amused themselves, and they liked boating, picnics—and music undoubtedly was a great thing.

McCulloch Sounds like an English Public School, doesn't it?

Hawkes Yes, and curiously enough, if you go across to the equivalent kind of civilization in the New World, they did invent a ball game, which our Bronze Age civilizations didn't. It is rather odd, that. It is the one thing in which they were more advanced and nearer to the present; but still, that's a small point.

The thing that always makes this kind of discussion so difficult is that one tends to assume always that one would have been born into one of the more fortunate classes. During the Bronze Age it was possible to rise in the social scale, but on the whole, people were rather stuck in their classes, so one's viewpoint would obviously very much depend on where one was born. There was also the question of which sex you happened to be. I think the whole question of women in the earlier civilizations is very interesting because, as I tried to suggest at the beginning, this was a fresh dawn, and everything was very spontaneous, and it seems to me that from these women, one can get some idea of what characteristics are innate, actually passed on in the genes, and sex-linked, and what are due to culture and could be readily changed.

In many ways I can see a very close resemblance between the twentieth century woman and the woman of the Bronze Age. I think one of the ways in which Women's Lib. have tended to be wrong is in assuming that, apart from the fact that we happen to be the bearers of life, we are almost exactly the same as men, and that what is called 'unisex' should be the ideal, both in what we do and what we feel. It seems to me quite clear that this is not so and that we have other psychological and physical drives which are clearly distinctive of us as females. I wouldn't for a moment though, underestimate the effect of culture, though there are certain innate qualities which seem to survive all cultural differences, and if you *do* look at the Bronze Age ladies, you get an idea that things haven't really changed very much, fundamentally. Their actual life is extraordinarily similar to our own; there is much evidence in letters and poems and especially in the laws, of passions (on both sides), and married affection, and, I am sorry to say, of married hatred. There is an interesting law that says if a woman hates her husband so much that she says, 'No, you shall not have me!' she can then have her dowry back and return home. That was quite enlightened. And then, of course, there was unfaithfulness, incest, rape; all such things occurred and were provided for. Again, the marriage situation was rather similar to our own, I think. It was monogamous, basically, but sometimes, as time went by, a second wife was allowed, and it was taken for granted that the man could have slave girls and concubines of various kinds. But I also suspect that certain allowances were made for the woman as well. There is a definite feeling of reasonableness in the laws, particularly in the arrangements made whereby widows or divorced women could be given money in order that they might have the 'man of their heart'. There is not much sign that most of the women wanted to go into professions or have an outside life.

McCULLOCH You mentioned our present problem of Women's Lib. Curiously enough, women seem to resent most being the object of men's lust, is that right? That is one of their great planks.

HAWKES Yes, but I would say on the whole, Women's Lib. are wrong there. There is obviously a great range of types, but I think the majority of women, now, as in those days, very much like the idea of being desirable, of being desired and pursued. There is a little verse from Sumeria, which illustrates this. It is very simple, of course.

> My beloved met me
> Took his pleasure of me,
> Rejoiced together with me,
> Made me lie on his honey bed . . .

And then there are a lot of endearments about the 'honey bed' and the 'honey man' and so on.

McCULLOCH So it doesn't look as if woman has really altered although there have been, of course, in the last hundred years, tremendous factors which have changed the whole relationship of the sexes. The easy assumption was, that a woman was not really capable of thinking. For so many thousands of years it was taken for granted by the male that she had no real faculty above her neck. Apart from a very few civilizations, she had no part, had she, in the real decision-making of the society?

HAWKES I have rather a strong feeling about this. I think, on the whole, it is only a percentage of women who really, positively, desire an outside life, to create things or to hold an important job, and that this again is one of the ways in which the Women's Lib. are wrong. Perhaps a maximum of twenty-five per cent really feel frustrated if they don't have that outlet. Now I get the impression that this was almost the same four or five thousand years ago.

McCULLOCH You mean that Barbara Castles and Margaret Thatchers were scarce in those days?

HAWKES No, I don't know that they were. It may have been more difficult to break through, and of course, where one is tremendously *with* Women's Lib. is that things should be made perfectly accessible and as easy as possible for all able women who really very much want to do something. But again, I do see just the same situation in Sumeria. You don't come across *many* women who were physicians or scribes, but you do find a few who managed to do it somehow. You also even find a few who were rulers. As you know, both in Sumeria and in Egypt there were women who, by ambition, managed to become the actual sovereigns, and this was accepted.

McCULLOCH What seems to emerge is that, despite the immense advance of our technology, the essentials of human life remain very much the same over 5,000 years.

HAWKES I do feel that, yes. But these old civilizations did have one characteristic which gave women an advantage—they were much aware of the opposites: night and day, land and water, man and woman, god and goddess. I think they gave absolutely full weight to the kind of generalizing that comes from women, call it the 'feminine principle' if you like. This is really where it seems to me that Women's Lib.—most of them—are so utterly wrong. They grossly undervalue this 'feminine principle', the smoothing things over and making life go on, and the feeling of unity with nature. To go *against* nature and create something out of it, is an essentially masculine characteristic. The feminine principle of peacefulness and unity with nature, and so on, is constantly being belittled today by women who seem in danger of resembling second-rate men, unless they are very careful. If Women's Lib. were in favour of the *right* thing, it should be heightening the importance of the feminine principle, instead of making women hobble along after the masculine one.

McCULLOCH You said that the male is always trying to escape out of the clutches of nature, and it is true, I think. He becomes abstract and airborne. Would you say that women's function is to hold man to the earth, to make him more aware of the actual environment in which he is?

HAWKES I think that was an important function, yes. And in a purely practical way you see women taking a big part in this present reaction against technology, and in favour of giving value to things on a more human scale.

McCULLOCH And then men are inclined to go too fast; they want to change everything quickly, and women are much more inclined, surely, to hold back and say, 'you can't do it at that speed'.

HAWKES I think, on the whole, we *do* do that. I would say, as a final thing, if you are considering past ages, as far as women are concerned, you might have a look at Bronze Age Crete, which is very different from the other two civilizations of that period. There is no doubt that the worship of the Mother-Goddess, which had survived from the pre-historic period, continued in this higher civilization and *there* the Goddess was supreme. Women were obviously equal with men in society but instead of wanting to work, or to wear sensible clothes or to be in any way competing with the men, they went to the absolute opposite extreme: the women dressed in a very feminine fashion, as I expect you know, lovely flounced skirts and tight bodices exposing their breasts. They were very provocative, and at the same time were able to do bull-fighting (or bull-playing) on equal terms with the men, if they wanted to. And the men, similarly, were dressed in a very masculine fashion, and the whole of that culture was light and airy and very brilliantly close to nature. For the first time in the world, there were wonderful paintings of nature, for its own sake, and none of this great glorification of hunting and warfare that dominated the other two civilizations. So I think Women's Lib. ought to be working for that kind of society, where the feminine principle was really lifted up.

McCulloch Do you take then a cheerful view of the symptoms of our time, especially in the relations of the sexes, of which many other people seem to take a gloomy view?

Hawkes I do, rather. It is a horrible, messy transition, and I detest a lot of the things that I see, and of course there are many dangers involved, but I do have a very strong feeling that a much better relationship of the sexes may be coming through. If so it is not really coming the Women's Lib. way, but more by this groping towards the spontaneous thing in both men and women.

30 March 1971

A visit from the Wykeham Professor of Logic at Oxford was bound to be regarded in the City as a special event as well as perhaps something like a descent from Olympus. It is widely supposed that academic gentlemen of such dizzy eminence are never to be drawn out of their rarified atmosphere into the lowly air of the money markets. But Sir Alfred Ayer consented to come, and a crowded audience had an exceptionally stimulating lunch-hour.

The B.B.C. 'Brains Trust' programme of happy memory had made the professor one of the best-known and effective communicators in the land. It was clear that the audience felt that although they had never seen him in the flesh, they were already in some sort of personal relationship with him. Whether or not they are quite certain what his function is, most people have seen him at work, seeking to elucidate problems of fact and meaning, and discussing the basic questions which our existence begs.

One popular illusion Sir Alfred Ayer has certainly done much to dispel, i.e., that a professor of philosophy is perforce a vague, absent-minded dry-as-dust individual, remote from the everyday world of common human affairs and interests, dwelling in a cloud cuckoo-land of abstractions and irrelevant ideas. I doubt if at any time he was ever anything like that, but his fascinating wife, Dee Wells would certainly have remedied it without difficulty or delay. In fact, Sir Alfred is as much renowned for his personal charm as for his brilliance of mind.

Among the Concise Oxford Dictionary definitions of the philosopher, is this gem, 'One who shows philosophic calmness in trying circumstances'. It will be seen from the dialogue that one philosopher faithfully lived up to that definition. This is all the more remarkable in view of the fact that, as we all knew, Sir Alfred is habitually and temperamentally more like a coruscation of intellectual fireworks than a placid sufferer of fools.

DIALOGUE WITH

Alfred Ayer

McCULLOCH I would like to talk to Professor Ayer about Man. And I think we might start, if I may, by asking you what your reflections would be upon the rather extraordinary article, which appeared recently in *The Times*, by the Provost of King's. In it he showed us that the scientist was the quasi-god of the modern world, and that he was very good at performing miracles, which was one of the functions of God, but that so far, he hadn't made out as the moral law-giver, which is what we really needed from the scientist. What do you think of that?

AYER Well, I hope the Provost of King's didn't say that the scientist was good at performing miracles, because, almost by definition, that is something a scientist never does. Anything a scientist does and establishes, becomes part of the order of nature and therefore excludes miracles.

I think the scientist has taken over one of the functions that was attributed to God, namely that of providing an explanation for the universe. Of course, even the scientist doesn't provide a *complete* explanation, but he does explain some things that previously, people in fear or helplessness, looked to God to do. As for the second function, of providing moral authority, I would say that the scientist is not equipped to do this, and I would also add that God was never equipped to do this either.

McCULLOCH But supposing we agree that someone should make moral decisions who should it be?

AYER I would say it had, in the end, to be the person himself, the individual. I think moral responsibility is something that is absolutely inescapable. One can, of course, put it off on to an authority. One can say, 'Well, whatever *he* says, I will do', but you, yourself, are still then taking responsibility for following this authority. I don't think you can ever escape this burden.

McCULLOCH But is it true that we are all equally capable of making moral decisions?

AYER We are not, of course, all *equally* capable. I mean, people have different experiences of life, different powers of reason, different judgements, and I think if one is faced with a moral problem it would be very foolish not to consult someone else. But, in the end, the responsibility has to be one's own. I don't think that any form of morality can be founded on authority. I regard morality as having mainly to do with communal living; with the effects of one's actions on the interests of other people, and almost everything one does, has these effects in greater or smaller measure. The thing is simply to try to arrive at a set of principles which one is prepared to stand by on all occasions. This is a laborious business and one has to seek advice, and of course, one can also derive one's principles from religious sources. I mean, it would be absurd to deny, for example, that Christianity—the doctrines attributed, rightly or wrongly, to Jesus—have had an enormous historical influence in forming people's moral attitudes.

McCulloch Would you say that your study of Jesus led you to any over-all principle which was paramount?

Ayer No. My studies of Jesus, I have to acknowledge, haven't been very deep. I was, of course, taught Christianity as a child at school, and read the Gospels, and have read a certain amount of comment and also some history.

I think it is very difficult to evolve, out of what you find, even in the Gospels, a single, clear and consistent moral code. If I had to extract any one single principle, it would be something not at all exclusive to the Gospels, something that you find, I think, in many religions, also occasionally among the Greeks, and that is the principle of altruism, expressed in rather crude form, that of doing to your neighbour as you would he should do to you. You have to assume that he is going to like what you like! But I think you can extract from this the principle that the other person has rights, that his views are to be respected and that you must come to some sort of accommodation. This seems to be the foundation of all morality. In a sense, of course, it is even a matter of self-interest in the end, because a community can only survive and a social life is only possible, on this assumption, that you do tolerate the other fellow.

McCulloch Yes. I find that statement extremely question-begging, the one about loving your neighbour as yourself, because I am not quite sure that I love myself as perhaps I should. I love something—you know—which is my comfort, my immediate self-interest, or whatever it may be, but whether or not that is myself. . . .

AYER I rather deliberately *didn't* say, '*loving* my neighbour as myself'. I avoided the word 'loving', it has nothing to do with it. I think it is preposterous to be told to love your neighbour. How can you possibly love all these numbers of people? I mean, it is absurd to say that you love everybody here. I only love a few people for special reasons. What is important is not *loving* but *respecting* your neighbour as yourself.

MCCULLOCH It is quite clear that you are not an actor, because I am sure an actor would say, 'I love you all!'

AYER At least actors can be convincing liars.

MCCULLOCH That depends on the quality of the acting! But to go back to this thing, would you not say that the problem of modern philosophy is still the question that has bothered all philosophers—what is the 'I' that says 'I am I', and what is its relation to the rest of the universe?

AYER I think this is indeed a question that has always bothered philosophers, and rightly, because I don't think anybody knows the answer to it. I don't at all claim that I do. It depends really on solving the mind-body question. I am easily identifiable as this particular body that has lived so many years on the earth, that follows a spatio-temporal path, and so on. But I am also something that is conscious, and the relation of the conscious part of me to this body, is something, I think, that hasn't ever yet been settled to everybody's satisfaction. It is still a philosophically disputed question.

There are those who believe that there is a total identity of consciousness with body, so that my mental states simply are states of my brain. There are those, at the other extreme, who think that there are two different substances, the body and the mind, the mind being a substance that persists after the dissolution of the body. There is a middle theory, a very uncomfortable one, which I hold. This says that mental states and bodily states are not identical but that the mind depends on the body, in the sense that it couldn't exist without it. I believe that, with the dissolution of my body, the series of my conscious states will end also. But I wouldn't claim authority for this view. This is what I, after considerable thinking about it, and not being able to answer all the problems, believe is the most probable.

MCCULLOCH But do we not suffer, perhaps, from an illusion that we are, so to speak, as individuals, much more solipsist than we really are? Is an individual quite so much an entity as he imagines himself to be?

AYER I think philosophers are apt to suffer from this delusion because of a purely philosophical difficulty. They are not quite clear how, from their own experiences, they can validly infer the existence of things outside them, and in particular, the existence of other bodies which are also seats of consciousness. But people who don't philosophise, as well as philosophers in their unphilosophical moments, are, I think, very keenly aware of their lack of isolation, of the fact that they are little units in a world which they don't control, subject to all sorts of pressures, and only one of a number of people of the same kind, affecting and being affected by the actions of others.

I think the danger is, not that we get too bound up in our individualities, but at the present time, that we make too little of them, and come to be regarded—by those who govern us, for instance—too much simply as social units, not as persons. I think the difficulties, the dangers, are really the other way.

MCCULLOCH Would the approach to a definition of the person, be 'the inter-subjectiveness of relationships'?

AYER No, this is not the definition of the person—I still think there is no way of defining the person except through continuity of the body. But it will serve as the definition of the objective world. I think the objective world is an inter-subjective world.

MCCULLOCH But isn't the inter-subjective world, as it were, a world that is to be distinguished from the objective world?

AYER No, the same, I would say.

MCCULLOCH You wouldn't think then that Büber was anywhere near the truth when he was talking about an 'I—Thou' world and an 'I—It' world?

AYER I am ashamed to say I don't know the works of Martin Büber, but from what you have quoted, I would say, no he wasn't right.

MCCULLOCH You would see the world as a unit, then, a unity, as *one* world? Yet you don't know what the world is. I can't help being reminded of the Oxford professor—I forget his name —who delivered a paper on the subject of the universe being one. And someone got up at the end of the lecture and said, 'Yes, I agree that the universe is one, but one *what*?'

AYER But does it mean anything, to ask if the universe is one or not, since the universe is, by definition, *one*? Since it is the universe it embraces everything and there can't be anything outside it. Asking what it is, can only, surely be asking what kinds of things there are in it, and what kind of relations they bear to one another. Now we don't know very much about the entirety of the universe, we don't know how it originated and it is still disputed in physics whether space is finite or infinite (the prevailing view is that it is finite). We know certain of its laws, we know a certain amount about the distribution of galaxies, the possibility of its expanding, though that, too, is conjectural. What we should do, I think, is not to ask these very large questions which don't have any very clear meaning, but try to make our questions precise, concentrate on precise issues and use scientific method. In this way we can try to advance our knowledge.

And so, what is the universe like? All right, read physics books, read chemistry books, read biology books. They will tell you a little—not all there is, obviously—and possibly, at some future time, read books of physiology and psychology, and then we will know what *we* are like.

MCCULLOCH You think that, scientifically, we could hope to get a full description of a human being?

AYER Well, what do you require for this? If it is going to be a sort of James Joyce thing, then clearly you are not going to get it. It took Joyce seven hundred pages to describe one day in Bloom's life in Dublin, and even then he must have left something out—though perhaps not much—so in this sense, no. But if you mean that one could get at the laws which govern the behaviour of human beings— yes, possibly. If we can get biochemistry making the bridge between biology and chemistry—I was going to say, between the organic and the inorganic—then if we could also get a unified physical theory—the sort of thing that Einstein wanted to do at the end of his life—and unify field theory and quantum theory, then you would have a very general statement of the laws that govern our behaviour. I would vouch that it is logically possible but I don't know whether it is practically feasible.

MCCULLOCH We must draw the conclusion, then, that a human being could be defined if we could get the various sciences to produce enough evidence. We would merely total the thing up: biology, chemistry, anthropology and so on, and, lo and behold, we have got at last a human being.

AYER I didn't say a human being could be *defined*—though I don't think the definition of man would present very great problems—but that his behaviour could be explained. I do think this to be feasible in principle, though I think it is an open question whether we can arrive at it. I think it is not impossible that one could construct a human being. The Frankenstein myth isn't entirely a myth. It seems to me that perhaps in two hundred years' time, they will be able to synthesize the materials in a laboratory, and so out of this would be produced a human being indistinguishable from those brought into the world in the classical way. I think that the behaviour of this terrestrial being, like any other terrestrial creature, could be, in principle, explained. However, until one can actually synthesize the materials, these are fairly empty claims, so all I am saying is, I see no logical difficulty of principle against it.

MCCULLOCH And would such a construction be able to produce moral decisions?

AYER Oh yes! This would be part of it, you see. If the test-tube product didn't have feelings, didn't have moral sentiments, one wouldn't have accomplished what one set out to accomplish; a synthesized human being would have to have the same powers, capacities, inclinations as we have. He would be able not only to reason, of course, which machines can already do, but also to have moral and passionate responses, which on the whole we think machines don't have. There is some doubt about this, you know, there are machines that cheat. There is a Japanese machine—the Dot-Play-Go-Bang—and it is supposed to say, 'My turn, your turn, my turn, your turn', but when it is losing, it says, 'My turn, my turn', and takes two moves. Well, that is already a first step towards becoming a human being.

MCCULLOCH Well, it sounds more like the *female* human being to me! This is very interesting. In other words we are, you would say, a kind of intelligent machine which is capable at the same time, of all kinds of varied moral decisions? This would bring in the whole question of value, would it not? This word 'value' worries me a little, in this context, because—well, why *are* some things worth more than others?

AYER I think all value is relative to a system of valuing, and that things are held to be worth more by some set of persons who attach value to them. In the last resort I don't think any answer can be given to your question, if what you require is that moral evaluation should be deduced from something else. What you can do is put down the factual reasons *why* you think something is valuable. In the end, I think, you have to just take your stand on moral principles and say, like Luther, 'I can no other'.

I suppose we are not the only creatures in the universe that make evaluations. I don't know how far animals do, but I think it is overwhelmingly probable that there is intelligent life elsewhere in the universe. If you consider the vast size of all the galaxies, it seems to me the probability is that, if not in this solar system, at least in some other galaxy, there are creatures on the whole resembling ourselves, and they will make evaluations too. Whether they will make similar ones or dissimilar ones, I simply do not know.

McCulloch Would you say that the question, 'What is it all for' has no meaning whatever?

Ayer Yes, I would.

McCulloch I thought you might! So that, in fact, here we are, rather interesting machines . . .

Ayer 'Machines' is very misleading, because it means we obey the laws of classical mechanics. We quite possibly don't.

McCulloch Oh, you think we don't? You think we may be more like buses than trams? I'm glad, if so, because isn't it what makes human life interesting, the unpredictability of the individual?

Ayer Ah well, here we are fairly safe. If what you want is the unpredictability of the individual, you are not likely, in practice, to lose it, because, for one thing, we are a long way yet from having a viable theory of the central nervous system. We haven't even got the viable theory of physiology, nor have we the dictionary which translates physiology into psychology. So that, in practice, our actions are likely to continue to be unpredictable, and we can hold on to our logically untenable—*I* think, untenable—notion of free will. As regards our practical life, nothing much is going to change even if all the scientific events that I am guardedly predicting, come about. Meanwhile I'm not going to predict what you will do, any more than I will predict what I am going to do, or our grandchildren, and that's a good thing.

McCulloch I want to ask one last question. Would you say then that modern philosophy is really making progress towards a solution of the problem of identity, the question of 'What am I?'

AYER Some progress, yes. I think we are a little nearer to getting the mind-body problem solved, but I think we are still far from having the final solution to it. I think we are a little clearer about problems of identity and also about the status of moral propositions and their relation to other forms of propositions. I don't think philosophy ever makes very startling progress. One of the handicaps of being a philosopher is that you never bring off tremendous *coups* like the physicist or the biologist, but I think in these central areas we are going a little way forward, yes.

18 March 1969

A friend not given to facile superlatives had told me that Sheila Hancock was a marvellous person. I was to meet her the following Tuesday when she was coming to do the dialogue. When I went to greet her on her way upstairs, I could see nothing to marvel at except a splendid hat which from my angle rendered her practically invisible. When we had met on more level terms, I did indeed see a great deal to admire besides a hat.

She has not the usual run-of-the-mill looks—item, two eyes, item, one mouth, etc. She is not assessable in terms of that kind of analysis. None of the beauty catalogue adjectives will do because your first awareness of her is as very much a distinctive person. Someone defined personality as courage in the face of life. But courage cannot stand by itself except as a necessary ingredient in the other qualities with which a person faces life in this world. When combined with intelligence, sensibility, fidelity, natural courtesy, humour and kindness, there is immediately recognisable an unusually real person. I do not claim that I saw all this the moment I met Sheila Hancock. All I knew then was that her friend had told me no more nor less than the truth.

Most people know what Sheila Hancock looks like from seeing her on the stage or the television screen, usually acting in situation comedies. She is a brilliant comedienne, and her gift of laughter has communicated to very many its power to relax the tensions and strains of modern life. But like others who master the craft of comedy, it is because she understands well Blake's profound insight when he wrote:

> Joy and woe are woven fine
> A clothing for the soul divine.

Her dialogue with me makes that abundantly clear.

My wife was in a hospital at the time, and after the dialogue she took me to the hospital and visited my wife with me. There was instant recognition by nurses and patients alike—the vibration of identity. To them also she was without question a marvellous person.

DIALOGUE WITH

Sheila Hancock

McCULLOCH I want to ask you what you meant by certain things that you said to a *Times* interviewer. It's not fair I suppose, but then Bernard Levin says that, being a parson, I do all the dirty tricks. Now, this is a fairly straightforward one, because you must have been reported accurately in *The Times*.

HANCOCK You're *joking*!

McCULLOCH Well, anyhow, the first one is a most interesting statement. You said, according to *The Times*, 'I find most things funny, otherwise I should find life tragic'. But aren't things both funny *and* tragic? If you turn something one way it's funny, but just tilt it round a bit and it's tragic. Do you think that is true?

HANCOCK Well, I suppose the truth is that I do find life tragic, and probably I use the fact of finding it funny as a defence. I'm inclined to look for the humour in a situation because I can't bear the tragedy. Take the basic slipping-on-a-banana-skin joke, which is the basis of a lot of comedy. Somebody breaking their neck on a banana skin isn't funny really, it's tragic. But, on the other hand, one laughs at it.

If I might give you an example of tragedy and comedy in my own life: it's a terrible story really. My husband died recently and the night he died, a friend was at dinner with us, and I was in a terrible state about everything, and this friend 'phoned the Registrar's Office and said, did I *have* to go to register my husband's death? And in fact they said I did; the next of kin had to go. So I went along and I must have looked like death, absolutely dreadful and desolate, and this friend went with me—quite a presentable young man—a friend of my husband's, I hasten to add. When we arrived at the Registry of Births, Marriages and Deaths, the Registrar recognized me and very kindly put me into the nicest room to wait, which also happened to be the room for getting married in. Then the wedding man came through the door and said, 'Right! Are you the happy couple?' Well, in the midst of my desolation, I fell about laughing because it was a ludicrous situation. And that is what I mean. I suppose I might have cried and said, 'How *dare* you! I am a widow!' and all that sort of thing, but it *was* funny. And I think in almost any situation you can find that sort of humour, and I think it's necessary to find it in order to survive.

McCULLOCH Now can I tell *you* a story? One Good Friday, I was coming away from church—I was Rector of Chatham at the time, which was a tough sort of place—and there was a chap, the drunkest man I've ever seen. Every time he stood up, he fell down and everyone was enjoying the joke. And then two chaps said to me, 'Well, if he doesn't get home soon he'll be run over, or something'. So we took him home. Now, it was a comedy all right; frightfully funny. But when we got to his home, a woman opened the door, and she looked at me and saw my cassock, and said, 'He's such a nice man, really'. Now what is that, comedy or tragedy?

HANCOCK Well, I find it tragic. I suppose it's funny too, but then all good comedy has an element of tragedy in it, just as all good tragedy has moments of comedy. If you can laugh at the most tragic moments in your life, it helps enormously, I think.

McCULLOCH But do you think there's something else, beyond both comedy and tragedy? Because when I put that drunk in the door I thought that there was something almost of mystery about it: how she could love him as she obviously did. Wouldn't you have thought that was a mystery?

HANCOCK Yes, well obviously there is an enormous element of mystery. I find life a constant mystery. I find it a mystery to find myself *here*! Because looking down the list of people you've already had here, I felt horrified because they all seemed people who were so sure of what they believed in. I am not sure of anything.

McCULLOCH Oh no! Mostly I have people who don't know what they believe in.

HANCOCK Well, you've had Lord Longford!

McCULLOCH Lord Longford is a very humble man and perhaps no humble man ever knows quite certainly what he believes in. I think he believes deeply, but because he's humble he doesn't like to say, and I think the public have got him wrong, very wrong.

Now Sheila, the second thing you said—which is very important to all of us, I think—you said, 'I am very sensitive at the moment to jokes which degrade women. I believe in the foundation of

Women's Lib.' But wouldn't you think that anything which degrades *any* human being is bad humour?

HANCOCK Yes, I would. All these quotes are always a sentence out of something I've said at much greater length. In fact, I've changed my opinion very much about humour against women. The Women's Lib. Movement I am sure would be very much against some of the things I do, as I often do series where I play tizzy, bird-brained women, and all the comedy comes from their stupidity. But when I analyse it, an awful lot of humour is based on that—Morecambe and Wise for instance. One of them is always an idiot. On the other hand I am a bit offended by jokes that look upon women purely as sex objects, dumb blondes. But the awful thing is that when you come to do humour intelligently, people don't laugh at it a great deal. I have tried, I really have, and the jokes don't go down as well. It's very difficult to find how we can laugh at women without being insulting.

You see, the reason that I am totally, I suppose, *for* Women's Liberation is for the men as well as the women. I care about men, women, black, white; and anything which discriminates against any human being I do object to. Now I am sure it's going to be better for men when women assume responsibility, help to pay the mortgage, and so on. But at the moment a lot of men, I think, aren't aware of that. They just see it as a threat. They've been brought up to believe that they've got to be the boss, and provide the living, and directly they don't do that there is a certain feeling of emasculation and they think, 'Oh God, I'm not fulfilling my role', just as a woman feels guilty if she is not fulfilling the roles that she has been brought up to believe are hers. But I can't help thinking that it must be right that we should share; it seems unfair that one or other of us should do everything. Men are very hard done by. Some women are intolerably selfish. I think poorly of the sort of woman who says she doesn't want Women's Liberation because she likes a man to pull her chair out for her, and carry her packages.

MCCULLOCH Forgive me, but I'm very much older than you and old-fashioned. I think carrying a woman's bag for her is part of a total relationship between the sexes which is fundamental—quite apart from the fact that a man is supposed to be stronger than a woman.

HANCOCK He's not!

MCCULLOCH Oh, of course he is! Sheila, we're not going to get through my four questions. Now, I'm moving on to your third quotation, 'We must have more and better facilities for the dying.' That seems to me a most important statement.

HANCOCK Yes, this is really something I'm trying to do in a practical way. Both my mother and my father have died recently: my mother, of cancer, like my husband. Cancer is a long-drawn out business and sometimes—not always, of course—incurable. The medical profession is geared to cure, because that is their training and when somebody is incurable there is, in some instances, a peculiar shutting-off. Probably some of you have had experience of this sort of thing, and the awful phrase that comes, 'I'm sorry, there's nothing more we can do for you'. Now there is a *lot* more they can do for you in terms of support, alleviating pain and . . . do you know Dr Cecily Saunders? Well, she runs a marvellous place called St Christopher's Hospice. She's a fantastic woman who has worked on drug control to the point where pain and suffering are reduced to a minimum. But unfortunately, the average general practitioner, I think, has only a very elementary knowledge of drug control. Then the facilities for home help are, on the whole, appalling. Again, they are trying to do something about improving the service, but if you are nursing someone at home, it is a frightening thing and you need help and support. I think this is the area where it's got to be done. It also involves a certain attitude towards death, I think.

MCCULLOCH Yes, there is something very bad about the modern attitude towards death. There is an art in dying. Perhaps that is something we've forgotten!

HANCOCK Well, it's something we've all got to do—like being born.

MCCULLOCH But birth is such a group thing, isn't it? You come into a world of people and family.

HANCOCK Well, death is the same, or it should be. You should go out of the world with your family round you; this is the ideal thing. Unfortunately, most of us are so frightened of coping with death—as I myself was—that one's instinct is to say, 'Oh, take them into hospital. *You* cope with it.' But, in fact, it can be the time when you become closest to each other, and can help each other. You need professional help too—drugs, people to help you with the basic medical care and that sort of thing, and that is what is lacking at present. Poor district nurses are rushed off their feet and they have too many patients. The Social Services need more money to increase their facilities.

McCULLOCH I liked what you told me your little daughter said about death. She's about five, isn't she?

HANCOCK No, she's eight now. Yes, well, when Alec died, I didn't really believe in life after death. So I couldn't, in all honesty say, as I think a lot of people say to children, 'Don't worry, you will see your Daddy later', because I didn't altogether believe that she would. So I said, 'I don't know, pet, I'd like to think we are going to see him again, but we none of us are going to know until we get there'. And then she said, 'Well, you know Mummy, it's going to be a great adventure—to see what happens'. So, you know, I think she is happy.

McCULLOCH Your daughter's remark is very like Athene Seyler's when she was in that pulpit. She said, being also an actress, that the thing she felt about death was that she would be so unrehearsed. Now what do you think about that?

HANCOCK Yes, I'm a bit worried about that too! I must say that the thing I most want to do is to die with dignity. I think the worst thing is to die in an undignified way.

McCULLOCH Don't worry, I think you'll die well! Have you got your 'famous last words' ready?

HANCOCK Oh yes, I've rehearsed all sorts of things. If I dropped dead now, I hope I'd think of something good to say.

McCULLOCH I was nearly killed once by a flower-pot—a geranium—coming off a third-storey window in Warren Street. I was on the way to meet my wife at Heal's and it was a very close shave indeed. I was terribly pleased when I got to Heal's because I had thought of the perfect epitaph, 'No more flowers, by request'. But, Sheila, what do you think she said? She didn't take the slightest notice of my brilliant witticism. She was very deflating and said, 'Didn't you go back? There might have been another flower-pot loose!' In other words, I had neglected to do my social duty!

Now, let's go on to your fourth statement which I think is the key to your personality; why you are so loved. You said, 'I've never been lonely. I like solitude and often spend hours alone to recharge my batteries.' You are never lonely, you say, meaning that you are not turned in on yourself and worried about yourself?

HANCOCK Well, I have a theory about loneliness, actually, though it isn't a new one by any means. Obviously some people who are lonely, are sick and can't make an effort, in which case it is our duty to look after them. But I think a lot of people are lonely because of selfishness: there are neighbours, people living in bed-sits, *somebody* who would be only too grateful for you to say, 'Come in and have a coffee'. Of course, you may get a rejection, but it's worth the risk. There are a lot of people who are lonely who don't need to be; I'm sure of that.

McCULLOCH You say you enjoy solitude; I share this. I think it is wonderful to be really alone for a bit, withdrawn and so on but I have found it is awfully difficult to enjoy solitude if you are terribly anxious about somebody else, somebody you love.

HANCOCK Yes, it is, but even then sometimes you need the time to sort out your anxiety. You see, I am a very muddled person and I sometimes get to fever-pitch with worry, often over infinitesimal things which I get out of proportion. Then you need to be alone, to sit quiet and say to yourself, 'Come on! Why am I worried, let's analyse it.' And sometimes I end up twice as worried as before! But I think you need to discuss with yourself sometimes, your motives and reasons and where you are going.

McCULLOCH Am I allowed to ask what 'yourself' is? 'Discuss with yourself', it is one of the most fascinating things, isn't it?

HANCOCK It's very boring in my case!

McCULLOCH Ah, now, do you remember the famous reply of the Oxford professor? He was always talking to himself, and an impertinent undergraduate asked him why he did. He said, 'Two reasons: first, I like an intelligent person talking to me and secondly, I like to talk to an intelligent person!' Now, I really thought you were going to tell us that you enjoyed talking to Sheila Hancock.

HANCOCK No, I don't enjoy Sheila Hancock at all. I find her pretty hideous. I am learning to accept her, which I didn't when I was young. Actually, I was sitting in the attic amongst the dust yesterday, turning out old diaries and letters, and it struck me, looking back to when I was younger, how obsessed I was with my inadequacies: there are pages and pages when I say, 'What am I going to do about my *nose*?' and, 'I couldn't possibly appear on television because I am so *grotesque*!' Now, I've just accepted that I'm inadequate, and it's easier to live with really. But I think that it is something which comes with age.

McCULLOCH Perhaps it is when you can accept your own inadequacy, far beyond yourself, that you find peace. The young are so desperate about the meaning of themselves, as you so brilliantly described, but there is a certain point in your life—if you really get faith—when you suddenly say, 'I am what I am'. I just mean, one becomes aware of a reality in which one exists and which is accepting one as one is, and is responsible, ultimately, *for* one.

HANCOCK Oh, but you see, that is why I *lost* my faith, because I found myself in a situation where I needed help and I thought, 'Right! I'll pray' and then I thought, 'Now, come on! I'm not sure that there is anybody listening to me.' It complicated the issue, somehow, to think that there was somebody outside, judging, either pleased with, or condemning, me. I was so tortured when I 'believed', finding an explanation for suffering. Now, I don't have to bother, it's just *there.* I don't have to say, 'Why does God allow that child to die?'

MCCULLOCH Curiously enough, I would say that in the second part of that statement you showed more faith than in the first part, because you no longer bothered in that introspective way about suffering, about this and that. All this stuff you talked about: 'when you were religious' and so on, meant, when you were trying to accept the formulae but you grow out of that. All people who are really religious grow out of the formulae, you know. One of the wisest things that was ever said was said by an Anglican divine in the seventeenth century, 'It were better you imagine what your religion is than what your Church is'.

HANCOCK Mmm! But where do you join? I mean, where do you go?

MCCULLOCH Very easy. If you're quite sure what your religion is, he went on to say, 'a religion that is true will be true for ever. But a Church can betray her trust.' In other words, if you can, accept the general outline of the Church, but don't get tied to formulae.

HANCOCK I think it's awfully difficult to do that. No, I couldn't go in and say, 'Yes, I agree with some, but I am not going to do this bit or that'. I'd have to have the sackcloth and ashes and be trailing around in bare feet if I joined, really.

MCCULLOCH Well, it *is* Lent. . . .

27 March 1973

No name is more bandied about in our time. It is not merely that Malcolm Muggeridge is a brilliant user of words, nor even that he could never be mistaken for anybody else. He has never licked anybody's boots, not even those of the many-headed Demos. On the contrary, so far from seeking to please, what he writes or speaks is nought for your comfort, and almost bound to enfuriate the complacent. And yet his name on an article or review will guarantee its being widely read; if he is to appear on a radio or television programme, the listening or viewing figures are sure to be higher than usual.

For most of his life an agnostic, and still a severe critic of the Church, he came to religious faith ten years ago, and has since consistently declared his conviction of the essential truth of Christianity. His detractors and disparagers accuse him of an unconvincing *volte face*, and often sound as if they feel that in leaving the company of the worldly wisemen, he has somehow let them down. They are highly suspicious that a man renowned for his intelligence and wit and, above all, a former editor of Punch, the most picric of satirists, a *bon viveur*, an outstandingly successful exploiter of the media, should in his sixties number himself among the simple-minded who struggle to transcend the world, the flesh and the devil.

In fact, to those who have known him personally, as in most conversions, the discontinuity is more apparent than real. The underlying motif of his life has been from his earliest years a deep distrust of the power structures of our civilization, and this found expression in the irony and satire of his writing. What he is saying now is not essentially different from what he has always been saying, that there is something rotten in the state of our civilization. The secular answer at the apolaustic level to the three main problems of the individual in society, those of sex, force and wealth, he always knew to lead nowhere. He kept looking for the clue to their effective solution and, like many others on the same quest, found that what was beyond him was already within.

DIALOGUE WITH

Malcolm Muggeridge

McCulloch Malcolm, somebody sent me a cutting from a newspaper which had a printed photograph of our rood-cross here. The cross is a very strange symbol, surely the most curious of any in the world that we are living in. When people ask me, as they do from time to time, what is the essential meaning of Christianity, I simply point to the rood and say, 'Well, that is really what it is all about'. Would you agree with that?

Muggeridge Oh, undoubtedly. Of course, it never ceases to amaze me that this particular symbol which, after all, is the symbol of a method of execution—it is a gallows, a scaffold—that this symbol, for the two thousand years of our civilization, should have inspired such an incredible amount of dedicated living, of joyous service, such an incredible pouring out of love. I think it is one of the strangest things in history. In a sense, I think, it says different things to different people, and says different things at different ages, in different phases of human history. But what I think, in all circumstances it says, is that what seemed in worldly terms a defeat, was a victory; what seemed in worldly terms, a death, was a resurrection; what seemed, in worldly terms, a scene almost of derision, in which a man—in the eyes of important people, a kind of crazy teacher—yet proved to be the new great light that had come into the world.

Having myself a great dislike for authority and power, and a strong sense that this is the pursuit which is most damaging to men and produces the most damaging episodes in history, the aspect of the cross I find fascinating are the words above it: 'King of the Jews'. That was put up as a piece of derision, as though to say, 'How can this miserable creature, whose crown is thorns, be regarded as a King of the Jews?' And yet, you see, what was happening in that scene was that all authority was henceforth going to be seen, in a certain sense, as derisory; that worldly power was never again going to be taken with complete seriousness. The pagan gods who were worshipped when that scene took place were all images of power, of sensuality. And they are also the gods of the new paganism today. But Jesus on the cross was revealing a different God, that embodied what is weak, not what is strong; embodied the notion of suffering rather than the notion of happiness.

McCULLOCH When you say that Jesus on the cross embodied what is weak, I take it you mean, weak in the worldly sense? Because of course, it proved to be the greatest source of power—spiritual power—the world has ever known.

MUGGERIDGE Oh undoubtedly. I mean, this cross is not particularly appealing today because the media on which we feed, for which I have worked, are saying something quite different from the cross. They are saying that happiness lies in getting everything you can; that happiness lies in self-indulgence, in being successful and rich and beautiful. And the cross says the opposite.

The cross means to me the ultimate reality. It means the ultimate truth about human life; something before which all the fantasies of the world are laid aside and in which one is confronted with the ultimate reality of one's existence. That reality is, as the Christian religion has taught, that in dying we live, in sacrificing we find ourselves, in loving to the point of forgetting this insistent ego inside us, we experience—and then only—the joy of life.

McCULLOCH Now this is curious, because most people in those days and in these, passed it by—the cross, I mean—because they thought it was life-denying. You are saying the opposite.

MUGGERIDGE Well, of course. You can take it as a rough and ready assumption that any contemporary jargon will be the opposite of the truth. When they say that the cross is 'life-denying' or 'sick', they mean that the way to live and to fulfil oneself is in seeking one's own happiness, one's own well-being, one's own fulfilment, through the ego, through the flesh, through time. Now, actually this is an impossible pursuit; this cannot be; and the whole of human history and everything that has ever been written in any book or play or delineated in any picture, to which we give the slightest attention, says the contrary.

McCULLOCH What you are saying, Malcolm, is that most people take the cross to be something about death?

MUGGERIDGE Yes, and of course it *is* about a death. It *is* a man dying but it was a man dying in order to be reborn; it was a man despising his physical existence to the point where he was prepared to sacrifice it for an eternal truth that he had seen and understood. That eternal truth has guided man through all the intervening centuries. He was dying because it was the only thing he could do; because it was the only way he could fulfil the purpose for which he had come into the world. He was dying in order that people might live; to show that the way to live is, in a sense, to die; that in dying to the self, to the ego, you are reborn.

McCULLOCH In fact, it wasn't about a death then, it was about life?

MUGGERIDGE Yes, but a new kind of life, a new fulfilment, a new joy, what St Paul called, 'the glorious liberty of the children of God'. Indeed, it is the only liberty that, truly speaking, exists.

McCULLOCH But to get hold of this you need to have a kind of—I don't know what—a poetic imagination or something, which the modern world doesn't think much of.

MUGGERIDGE I don't think of it as poetic imagination, it is more an awareness of reality, which is what the contemporary world lacks because it is fed on fantasies—scientific fantasies that man can shape his life in such a way that he is a kind of god, believing that he can do anything by himself, can control his environment and so condition himself and his fellows that he, a mortal man, can live in this world with supreme contentment and equability. Now, that is untrue. But this is the fantasy that is propagated. Now the cross represents reality; it tells us that we can't do those things, that we are nothing except in relation to our creator.

McCULLOCH Isn't it strange, though, that this particular event did so much; actually changed the course of history?

MUGGERIDGE Well, of course. It is the most remarkable thing that has ever happened. It is an extraordinary thing that an obscure man dying, should completely transform human life and the things people hope for, the things they attempt to achieve. Now it may be that, historically, in the Western world, that is all over, but if it is over then the Western world will collapse, because that is what it is based on. *This* is its symbol, it is under the aegis of this symbol that it has created a civilization, a law, relationships between men, a culture, art, literature—all these things.

McCULLOCH But most of our modern contemporaries think that this is sheer foolishness.

MUGGERIDGE They think it is ridiculous, but then would you say, if you look around the world, if you look here in London, that they are making a particularly good job of providing a way of life for people today?

McCULLOCH I think the twentieth century has had a dirty trick played on it. It has lost its myths. It doesn't understand that behind the scientifically observable world, there lies a huge area of experience upon which science, by its very terms, cannot throw light. I think the modern world has been betrayed, because the whole grandeur of the Christian revelation of truth cannot come inside its mind, because its mind has been closed to anything that can't be proved: like at what temperature water boils, or something.

MUGGERIDGE Well, I agree that science is a colossal con-trick. It has managed to produce a lot of prizes, but it hasn't illuminated life.

McCULLOCH But the *honest* scientist—of whom you and I know a few—doesn't say this is what they ever thought they would do.

MUGGERIDGE That is true. Perhaps, from the point of view of how people live, the greatest importance of the cross is that it generates the one virtue most lacking in the world today—humility. When you stand before that cross, your bluff is called, your pretensions are exploded. You are not what you would like to suppose yourself to be—a person of exceptional intelligence, or charm, or this or that; you are just one man among all mankind, looking at this symbol, first of the frailty of a man, and then of the majestic truth that came into the world through that frailty.

McCULLOCH You see, most of us, Malcolm, want to be a great success before we die because we, in the modern world, think that death is probably, almost certainly, the end. So we have only got this small link of time in which to get what we most want, or to make the most of what we've already got. We are all rushing against time. What light, do *you* think, the cross throws upon death?

MUGGERIDGE The cross not only throws light on death, but, in a certain sense, it abolishes death. The point is that the people who actually watched Jesus die thought that that was the end. It was the Christians who came after who showed that it was the beginning, and that it would never be possible, in the light of that cross, to believe that death was an end.

McCULLOCH This of course is the essential meaning of Easter. People have always liked to come to church on Easter Day. But the interesting thing is that lately there are more people very often in church on Good Friday than on Easter Day, even. Would you say that was a hopeful sign?

MUGGERIDGE I think anything that brings people out of bingo halls or looking at television, or reading the papers and all the other imbecile things on which one spends a great deal of time, and into a church, to *look* at a cross, is in itself good. It is also my impression, as an old journalist, that increasingly this notion of producing a kingdom of heaven on earth through an ever rising gross national product, and laws, and all these different things, is beginning to look very tattered in the eyes of many people, especially the young. They feel it is not working out.

MCCULLOCH Could it be that what they are really looking for is the life—the truth—behind the ancient myths? The trouble is, people today tend to think a myth is a sort of fairy-story, whereas in fact it is a deep truth, expressed in the form of a story. The old myths, if only they knew it, really reflect something they want.

MUGGERIDGE I agree! I think they *are* looking for truths but I think they realize, in a vague way, that the various instruments for persuading them and instructing them, have nothing to do with truth.

MCCULLOCH Do you think that, on the whole, the instruments you mention—which are called 'media' and don't mediate—do you think they are in the hands of people who think that scepticism—disbelief—is the only thing to put over?

MUGGERIDGE In a way I would regard that as hopeful. My belief is that they are in the hands of people who simply have no coherent purpose of any sort. They simply have this machinery of persuasion, this screen to fill, these sheets of newsprint, these hours of radio time, to *fill*. All they know is that there are lots of viewers listening, eyes looking, minds requiring, this particular *pabulum* that the printing presses produce. And they deliver it. The number of them who have got any sort of purpose—even an evil purpose—is very few. Indeed it would be very agreeable to think that there *was* a wicked conspiracy to delude us all with this great machinery of persuasion so immeasurably more powerful than anything of the kind that has ever existed, because then we could get rid of the conspirators and make use of it. But the *shallowness* of it and the falsity of it, believe me, are built into the medium itself, and therefore it is only in detaching oneself from all that and looking up at a cross that it is possible to discern what the true meaning of life really is.

McCULLOCH But I suppose that, despite everything, all the people who read the papers, look at the box, are faced, at certain times, with the problem of suffering, and I cannot see that anything in this world so far has offered a more convincing answer than the cross. Nor ever will. But it isn't an answer that you can scientifically measure, is it?

MUGGERIDGE No, but it makes it all comprehensible, it makes it possible to understand why it should be in the very experience of living to suffer. If Jesus hadn't suffered, there would have been no Christianity; if we didn't suffer we shouldn't be alive. And yet, you know, there are some scientists who have the naivety to believe that it might be possible to take all suffering out of life. You would do various things through euthanasia, kill off all the people who were physically imperfect or senile or imbeciles, then, through genetics, you would breed people to be healthy, beautiful, intelligent and so on. Of course, it is a nonsensical idea, but if ever that idea were to be fulfilled it would be the most demeaning thing that had ever happened.

McCULLOCH If you were to take suffering out of the world, I presume you would have to take love. You couldn't possibly have a world in which love was a possibility *without* suffering, could you?

MUGGERIDGE No, exactly, because you would take away from human life that very capacity to identify yourself with someone else, which is the magic that love and suffering, through the cross, propounds to human beings. That is the whole point.

McCULLOCH Here is something which I would like to have your thoughts on. I remember Alec Douglas-Home saying, in the pulpit there, that the problem really was, in these days, that people are no longer accustomed to thinking, before they do something, 'How will this affect others?' I think that we *were* drilled—at any rate, to some extent—to think before we acted, and to say, 'What will this mean in the lives of other people, if I do it?' But people now seem to have the curious idea that they can act in a vacuum. Do you think this is so?

MUGGERIDGE I think it is, yes, in a general way. If you want me to generalize, I think that that, and all the other things we have said, really relate to the same thing, that is, that people today are really trying to make life work out within the dimensions of their own mortality and fallibility. This is, of course, impossible.

McCULLOCH I agree, but how would you show somebody who was bewildered and confused, as so many are today—how would you point them in the direction that the cross, in your experience, points?

MUGGERIDGE I think it *is* very difficult because our Western world is going through a phase of trying to live in materialist terms, and in materialist terms the cross has no place. But of course the only way that you can tell them about it is through the gospels and epistles, through the story of Christendom, which is the story of the cross. They don't listen, and I suspect that in the years to come they may well listen less and less, certainly in our part of the world.

McCULLOCH You say they don't listen, but don't you feel there are signs that they are beginning to listen more than they have done for possibly two generations?

MUGGERIDGE Well, I think there *are* signs, yes. There are always people—perhaps many more than we think—who don't accept the illusions of our age and who see that the cross and all it symbolizes, alone provide an answer to the appalling dilemma of living in the twentieth century. There will always be the few who refuse to accept mortality as the total dimension of their lives. But, on the other hand, there will always be times when the expression of faith is muted. Today is such a time.

We might have lived, say, in the fourth century when Augustine lived, and we might have been some very enlightened, liberal Roman. In that case we would probably be trying to understand what was going on, and we would reach the conclusion that our particular civilization had passed its prime, was declining and might easily succumb to the barbarians. Probably we wouldn't have thought of the cross as representing the true alternative. But it did. That whole majestic pagan world disappeared—and we go now and scrabble about to find bits of masonry and rubble. And Christendom was what replaced it. So today, when once again it looks as though, in earthly terms, our way of life is foundering and the structures of our civilization have become very groggy, well the cross is there still, and maybe some other new fantastic demonstration of what it is saying will occur.

28 March 1972

Journalism is an umbrella word to cover many kinds of writing, most of it today fit only to be consigned as quickly as possible to the waste-paper basket. But above this ruck of journalese-purveyors there is an élite who adorn the profession with writing which has both wit and style. To this distinguished few Katharine Whitehorn undoubtedly belongs, and her essays, both grave and gay, are brilliantly done and widely read.

The wit and the style of her writing are the woman herself, the stamp of her personality. Because she is frequently to be seen in television discussions and heard on radio, many know her well as a very attractive woman who can speak her own mind with force, clarity and humour. They know well the level grey eyes with the smile behind them, the generous mouth, the low-pitched voice, the sheer lively intelligence of her approach to the entire farrago of human affairs. As I know her, she is fundamentally a happy person, and capable of taking the slings and arrows with fortitude as well as enjoying hugely the smiles of fortune. I guess that she is capable of swift rages, though I have only once been on the receiving end, I think meritedly, when I had said something particularly fatuous. She is blessed with two marvellous parents, and a very satisfactory marriage. In fact, she is an enviable woman with many gifts and graces.

But what my wife and I love most in Katharine is that she can burn not so much with righteous indignation as with genuine compassion. She is no less aware of the tragedy than of the comedy of our human situation, though she has the wisdom to recognize that there are no easy answers. She is no bluestocking in the sense that her academic and intellectual ability leaves her on the sidelines, detached and uninvolved. Her best writings and utterances reveal how deeply she cares about the unnecessary frustrations and sufferings which man's inhumanity and stupidity inflict on his fellows.

DIALOGUE WITH

Katharine Whitehorn

McCulloch Some time ago, in the *Observer*, on the page which is now probably as lively a page in the press as there is, you had a letter which fascinated me. It was from a woman who had lost her husband and had the experience of suddenly finding that her very closest friends tended to leave her alone, and those that did come seemed poised for flight. She couldn't make out why, and it was the loneliest period in her life. This, I thought, was a most important letter. Why were they like that?

Whitehorn This woman thought that people were embarrassed by her because she was grieving, and also that they had the feeling that she was in some way *bad luck* because she was a widow. I think other letters we have had since then, and also the author who provoked this article, say that it is a characteristic of nowadays, that the whole idea of death is taboo; it is the thing you can't talk about, just as sex used to be. Nowadays people talk about sex all the time, but get embarrassed talking about death: about people who have died. And especially are they embarrassed if they have to cope with people who are grieving for someone who has died. It's as though we have swept this one under the carpet, that it is unmentionable. If you don't talk about it you can pretend it isn't there and it won't happen to us.

McCulloch And is this true of a lot of other problems that we don't really like? For instance, the thalidomide baby?

Whitehorn Well, I would say that it is. In a way, we have been encouraged to think that all the inadequate people are taken care of by experts, and that is another way, I suppose, of sweeping it under the carpet—pretending that people who are a little weak in the head 'would be far better off, wouldn't they dear, in a home?'

McCulloch This could go for many others, surely: spastics and people with curious ailments and the deaf? We just don't want to have to face the fact that some people are carrying a bigger burden than we are, far bigger. We don't want to be tied up with it. Why is that?

WHITEHORN Obviously every age has felt an obligation to be something or other, whether nice or nasty, but generally speaking, I think that in the days when life was genuinely tougher and more miserable, it was felt that you had an obligation to do the nasty thing, though you would really much prefer to do the pleasant thing. Nowadays you feel that you have an *obligation* to be happy and well-adjusted, to have good relationships and a fulfilling job and all that kind of thing, and you feel a failure if you don't have it.

McCULLOCH But isn't it strange that in this present age, all these things that you say are objectives, are not fulfilled? Take good relations, for instance, I would have thought, reading the novels—even of the Victorians, who are so disparaged—they seemed to have better relationships, on the whole, than the people today.

WHITEHORN I don't know. I wouldn't like to pronounce on that. I think they sat on a great many more of their miracles than we would be prepared to sit on. I can never make up my mind whether you do or don't go some way towards coping with your difficulties by saying, 'Well, they can't be helped'. I've often had a theory that pepole who consider themselves to be irrevocably married, don't make quite such heavy weather of problems and crises that arise as people who are saying to themselves all the time, 'Oh goodness, was this marriage a mistake? Perhaps we might divorce; perhaps we *should* divorce!' I think that if you simply soldier on, putting one foot in front of the other, some problems go away, but I think a lot of other problems may perhaps be made much worse.

I would not like to say that the Victorians were happier than we were but I think they recognized that everybody's life included doing a whole lot of things that were not supposed to be fun, but were—you know—this great, gaunt word 'duty'. The idea was usually used as a stick to beat somebody else with—married women telling their unmarried sisters that of course it was *their* duty to stay at home and look after mother. But at least, I think, in those days either you were having the life you wanted or you felt you were doing the right thing. Nowadays, if you are not having the life you want, you feel in the wrong as well. I think that accounts for people's reluctance to admit to the nasty things;

to deformed children and to the facts of handicap and deafness and even death.

McCULLOCH I want to take up the word 'duty'. Has it no relation to love? You know—'Owe no man anything but to love one another', which is one of the great statements of the world, I think.

WHITEHORN I think it is one of the soppiest. The world is full of people who are supposed to be radiating love, but they don't actually *do* anything.

McCULLOCH Ah, I think this is the nub of what we are talking about. It is not simply a question of *radiating* love, that's all bilge. Love is a very stern, hard act of will on the part of the individual. You said marriage is this, that and the other, but it seems to me that if you depend upon a sort of feeling which is called love, you crash heavily.

WHITEHORN Well, I'm sorry, we do in fact agree. I thought when you said, 'only that we should love one another', that this was all. I think the word 'love' means what you are prepared to *do* about it.

McCULLOCH Well, that is duty, isn't it?

WHITEHORN I think you can really set this up two ways round, can't you? You can say, if you do your duty by someone for long enough, doesn't that amount to a form of love? But I wouldn't say that there was no such thing as a duty that was useful even though you didn't have any warm loving feelings about it at all. I mean, I think there are a lot of things that have to be done, and I'm thinking now not so much of the marriage context, as looking after older people, where it really *is* duty and only duty which keeps you going—at least for a time. But I don't think it is useless if, for maybe a stretch of years, you don't actually feel any appropriate emotions about it at all. I think, in a way, this is something that one learns from religious disciplines. They say, 'Well, never mind what you feel about this, just do it, that's the point'. And the fact that you could probably make life bearable for your slavering old aunt, even if it was very nearly unbearable for yourself, I think is something you have to face up to and say, 'It's my misery and her slight remaining pleasure or satisfaction'. You can't get off the hook by saying, 'If I do all this without really caring for her, it is worthless'. Unfortunately, it isn't worthless.

McCULLOCH 'Unfortunately'—that's the operative word. You see, it is a curious thing about the modern age, that if you are in pursuit of earthly felicity, anything that interferes with that pursuit is regarded as too difficult and is, in your phrase, swept under the carpet. I mean, if there are thalidomide babies, or if a woman has a husband who goes and dies, well that is just too bad, we don't want anything to do with it. If somebody is totally deaf, we don't want to be bothered about speaking to them, and so on. We had a beautiful creature here not long ago, who was very unhappy because she had not heard from her young man. She was a spastic and the young man had not written to her. She was very unhappy. We just want to avoid this sort of problem, you know. What is in us that makes us do that these days?

WHITEHORN I should think the impulse to avoid the unpleasant has always been there.

MCCULLOCH I'm not sure you are right about that. In large cities, maybe, but I would have thought that they were much kinder in small communities—in villages and so on—and they still are. Where there is a particular problem like a spastic or a totally disabled person or even a mongol, a village will show far greater kindness on the whole—you will contradict me at once, but I think so—than in this vast impersonal metropolis that we all like to live in.

WHITEHORN Well of course, it is far easier to avoid getting mixed up with the unpleasant in a large place, but I'm not sure about villages. There is a brutish element in people which you have to be a very sentimental arcadian to think is not present in ordinary village life. Certainly village life *used* to be very tough indeed, and I think they were cruel too, but probably in a different way. The old and the tiresome were kicked around and sworn at and starved, but at least they still belonged. The sense of isolation and of not belonging is what drives a lot of these people today to form small societies and particular handicapped groups—two new ones start up every week—because the only way they can find proper comradeship is to find other people like themselves.

I know particularly this question of the isolation of the deaf, because my mother, whom you know, is totally deaf and the awful thing is that people find it easier to assume that somebody who is deaf is also stupid, than to go through the perhaps *slightly* tiresome business of saying whatever you say very slowly and clearly. And I've noticed often that charities for the blind have no difficulty in doing well because everybody can at once imagine themselves blind. With the deaf it's much harder, it is a question of keeping in touch, in friendliness, with them, through what is in fact, a language barrier. It is like having someone who is perpetually in a state of not knowing English. You know you can stand this for a short time, but if a person is deaf it's like this for ever. And with spastics too—it's not a nice, easy thing, helping a spastic. It's a question of going on being understanding when circumstances are really difficult. Parents who have got autistic children, who are often a fair bit of social nuisance, find that their friends just can't take it. They don't actually say in so many words, 'We will never have the Joneses round again because they have a difficult child', because that would be a rather lousy thing to say. What they do is just put off having the Joneses round, or have them on an occasion when they can obviously only be asked *without* the child, so there is a good reason for not including the difficult person in.

McCulloch Do you think it would be better for us to lump it all off on to the State? Because we could get on with our search for earthly felicity then, and not be bothered. We put our two bob—ten pence in whatever it is and leave it to them. How would that be?

Whitehorn Well, I think there are two meanings in what you are saying. I think obviously in one way you have to say, 'No, of course not', because the State can only provide the material things and it isn't *just* material things these people need. What I do wish is that the obligation could be spread a little thinner. I don't know if you feel this but it seems to me, among my friends, that there are one or two very harassed and dedicated people who seem to be attending to practically every difficult person in the neighbourhood and most of the rest do nothing at all. I am sufficiently wedded to the concept of earthly felicity, as you put it, to think that it is very rough that anybody who hasn't a tremendous vocation should be asked to cope non-stop and all the time with these problems; and that most of us could do a little bit more to take the strain off it. But the trouble is, as things are, the one or two people who *are* aware, carry the can for everybody and then—you see this sometimes—someone who has lived entirely for other people for ten years, suddenly says, 'I can't stand it any longer', and drops the lot.

McCulloch Yes! You know, I have been a parish priest for a long time—before I came here, which is a different kind of parish—and it was quite true that if you got that kind of a jam in your parish, you went to the same people. You went because you knew perfectly well you would get an affirmative answer, 'I'll go and see them; I'll go and do something for them'. And the terrible thing in this country at the moment—you are quite right—is that a tiny group, comparatively, of the population are doing anything about anything. I saw the figures the other day and you hear all the things said about the churches which, goodness knows, are very often justified, but it is an astonishing thing that seventy-five per cent of the voluntary work done in this country is done by the churches which are only about ten per cent of the population. You can work that out for yourselves. This is the problem, this is where it hurts—to look around and know that there are an awful lot of people—of good people, too—but the moment you say, 'Here is Mrs X who's got a handicapped child', you have only got about three who will actually volunteer to do anything about it.

WHITEHORN I wonder if—I'm thinking as I speak, which is a bad idea anyway, but—well, I remember John Crosby writing a very funny piece saying, 'Oh, here's another group that I am suddenly supposed to feel guilty about'. There does tend to be an enormous amount of guilt about the things that society does wrong, but the snag is, as soon as you step over the line and become one of Those Who Help, then you have *all* the world's burdens on you. If we could have a Community Guilt—you know, on the principle of the American charities (they have a Community Chest and you pay all your money into this)—then everybody could take a small share, so that parcelled out between the lot of us, the whole thing would be more *manageable*. After all, even your three marvellous, church-going women who will look after anybody, still want a bit of normal life. I wonder if perhaps belabouring people about how escapist they are being, doesn't in some way force them to be more escapist; they feel that if they once get into your clutches they will be worrying night and day about the really sickening and insoluble problems. If they were allowed to give a *part* of their life to this, but not the whole thing, they might be more amenable. But I have no experience of recruiting people in this way, so I may be wrong.

MCCULLOCH No, I'm sure you're right! What you have said reminds me of an American utterance which I picked up last time I was in the States. Somebody said to me, 'We've got to organize ourselves to love our neighbours'. Do you think, perhaps, that the trouble is, we try to do too much as individuals and therefore tend to overlap and to waste potential energy and so on? Maybe the American was right and we *should* organize ourselves into helping-groups. Or is it a question, not of 'either or' but of 'both and'?

WHITEHORN Yes. There's so often a split, isn't there, between the people who say, quite rightly, that giving the odd bob to Oxfam and making one or two moist-eyed visits to an old folks' home twice a year, will never achieve a fraction of what, say, a Government aid system like Social Security can do, which is true. And those who say that any official agency can be inhuman and rigid and that they're no substitute at all for a shoulder to cry on or a spot of help sorting through the darned regulations. Quite apart from the fact that if it's anything to do with overseas aid, there are always political or commercial complications of some sort. And the trouble is, they're both right. I mean, you never get a proper aid system unless it's backed by government—and a reasonably uncorrupt government at that—but half the people never seem to get even what help they're entitled to.

The most hopeful thing I've noticed is that people under thirty are so much more involved than my lot were. My *parents* were involved, they took in a refugee in the thirties and sent socks to displaced persons and what-not; but my postwar lot just wrung their hands about the inadequacy of their own motives and never did a darned thing. Now I hardly ever meet a with-it young person, or whatever you'd call it, who isn't visiting in Pentonville or working two evenings a week for *Release* or going on a hunger walk for Shelter. They know the State doesn't do the lot—and I think that's healthier.

7 November 1972

Nobody could carry off world-wide fame more quietly or with less concern. For several years ahead he is always committed to musical engagements in many countries. Honours fall thick upon him, by no means least the knighthood conferred upon him by the British Sovereign. But never was anyone less like a panjandrum. He is no actor; so, even if he tried, he could never appear pompous or self-important. He is the same quietly-smiling, friendly man, whether he is in a private house or on a public concert-platform.

No professional life is more constantly arduous than that of a great *virtuoso*. The self-discipline required is as relentless as that of a member of the strictest religious order. From childhood Yehudi Menuhin has submitted to an exacting rule of life in order to perfect the quality of the music he was born to make. Yet within that inexorable discipline, and indeed by means of it, he is the happiest, freest, most relaxed of men, as well as one of the most deeply spiritual. What he communicates is the knowledge of the things which make for our peace, and the truth to be found in the things of beauty.

What he has seen in the many countries he has visited has made him passionately concerned to work for the removal of the artificial barriers which separate man from man. Wherever there is flagrant injustice or brutal cruelty his voice is added to those who denounce it. His patriotism, if it had to be expressed, would be a passion to realise the vision of that other country of which Cecil Spring-Rice wrote, 'Her ways are ways of pleasantness and all her paths are peace.'

Many recognize Yehudi to be a seer and mystic. It is certainly true that his inward vision is wonderfully clear, and he is unmistakably rooted in the life of the Spirit. But he knows that other world as the immediate enrichment of this world. For that reason he has a rare capacity for enjoying this life at depth and in simplicity. Most of all, he enjoys a marvellous companionship with his ballerina wife, Diana, whose brilliance and wit are his constant delight.

DIALOGUE WITH

Yehudi Menuhin

McCULLOCH I have always thought of Mr Menuhin as, not just the citizen of any particular country, but as a citizen of the whole world. Just at present the world is obviously in a very strange and difficult state. I believe that it is because we are omitting a certain aspect of man. Men are regarded, more and more, as consisting of just a body—a physical apparatus and a brain—and I feel that we are missing out somewhere a most important aspect of ourselves. What do you feel about that?

MENUHIN I agree entirely. The very fact that we ask ourselves questions, that we wonder where we are going, why we are here, where we have come from—that we are concerned with these things, is proof of this other element which suffuses us all the time. And we have the faculty that enables us to see ourselves from a distance, as it were. For we are not only what we are at this moment, we are what we were for millions of years, we are what we will be, and even in terms of this moment, we are, in a sense, everything—in that we are connected with everything. We would not be able to go to the moon, we wouldn't be able to delve into the mysteries of nature, unless we had this feeling that these mysteries somehow belong to us and we belong to them. I feel that unless we regard ourselves, not only in our own narrowest interest, but as the carriers of the past and as responsible to the future, we are not really being true to ourselves. More and more do we need to be aware of the spiritual sense in everything we do. We cannot afford to do any job, however big or however small, without realizing this spiritual element in it.

McCULLOCH Would you say that there was something spiritual in commonsense?

MENUHIN Yes, very much so, because commonsense is that ability to think which takes into account all the dimensions of the senses, and the past and the present and the future, and all the rest—that is commonsense. The Germans, for instance, if one can generalise, are wonderful at intellectual constructions which so often lack commonsense. The fact that you can build an intellectual structure of great complexity on a false premise, is known to everyone. In fact, we all build, each in his own prejudiced way, great constructions of justification of our own behaviour on false premises. We say, 'I did that because I meant well' or 'because I couldn't avoid it' or 'because someone forced me to do it' or 'I was *conditioned*', and so on, and these are all good reasoning on false premises.

Commonsense, which is a combination of reasoning plus instinct is the computer sense inbuilt into every human being. Instinct is the repository of experience, of thousands of years of past history and of hundreds of minutes in our own life. That experience is reduced to instinct because—well, when I play a work, and I am interpreting it, I am not going through with my conscious mind, every smallest motion I do, and every smallest inflection, nor am I, while speaking to you now, looking up each word in the dictionary. If I were, I would, undoubtedly, learn a great deal, but you and I wouldn't have any communication. Therefore a great deal of what is happening at this very moment is governed by habit, instinct and commonsense, I would hope!

McCULLOCH Indeed—I am absolutely marvelling at this, because it seems to me the most commonsense explanation of the job I am trying to do that I have ever heard. The point is that we are all under the influence of far greater powers than we ordinarily are aware of and, presumably, to become more ourselves we have got to become more *aware*, in the widest sense. Is that right?

MENUHIN Aware, and *resigned* in an enlightened way, because as we are in the hands of great powers which are quite beyond us, we cannot hope to dominate them, but we can hope to play along with them, ride the torrent, just as a good swimmer cannot hope to annihilate the water, but lives with the water, with its temperatures and its currents. I think, very often, of something which has been sent on its way, like a gesture, say, or if you are a golfer, you drive the ball a long way and the ball, while it is travelling—even if it were conscious of where it was going—couldn't alter the direction in which it has been sent; in the same way, we are living on a certain wave of momentum, we are being carried along by the momentum of the past, by our own habits, our civilization and society. We don't know where we are going, but if we have faith in our ability somehow to cope with whatever situation arises, if we have a certain trust in relationships, and so on, we will probably carry along. But this element of resignation and faith is just as important as the element of domination and control.

McCulloch Tell me, we have a tremendous sense of freedom, or desire to be free. Is this a spiritual thing?

Menuhin Yes, I think it verges even on the mystical because it is a proof of the need for union with the All. As we cannot be free individually—we cannot possibly, any of us, do absolutely anything that comes into our minds—that freedom we are speaking of is a freedom that comes of harmony with our environment and with those around us. We are free so long as we behave in a way that maintains that harmony but as soon as we behave in a way that *doesn't*, we are no longer free. So that that freedom is first of all a freedom of the heart, of the imagination, which begs for union with the All, so as to find that freedom which ultimately only exists in complete subordination.

McCulloch In other words, are we free because we begin to understand the way the universe works? I mean, if we go against the way the universe really works, we are obviously abusing freedom, aren't we?

Menuhin Yes, freedom is very relative and we are free so long as there isn't a sense of crude compulsion. We can say, within reason, what we want to say—and that is something we bless this country for—provided, again, we don't go beyond the bounds of courtesy and respect for those elements which are held in common and to which we pay respect in common. I think that is very important because as soon as one destroys any kind of common point of respect or the understanding of the basic need for courtesy, all freedom is lost.

McCulloch 'Courtesy'. May I pick up that word? Because, do you think that courtesy is a sort of basic thing in the universe itself?

Menuhin Well, my wife has two very good things she says about it. One is that she believes courtesy must be in the circumference. She speaks of 'lateral courtesy' as well as courtesy head on, so to speak. And she also calls courtesy the oiling, the lubrication of society, and that is perfectly true. Otherwise you rub against each other, you rust, you break edges off, you lose a lot of energy and waste time. Courtesy is a tremendous lubricant and as such should be cultivated with all the care and attention it deserves.

McCulloch Now I want to change slightly the subject, not very much, but do you think the young of today have woken up to the fact that we are ignoring the spiritual state of man, and, for all their mistakes, *they* are trying to find it?

MENUHIN Oh, very definitely so. Only they are determined not to find it in the embodiment of anything which was, or pretended to be, spirituality in the past. I think they may get over this purely childish reaction, provided the embodiment of past spirituality—that is, our various Churches—are willing to accept that certain elements in the dogma, have to be changed, too, in order to be in harmony with the present world. For instance, the fact that spirituality belongs not only to man but that there is an element of it in everything, including animals. And then the other thing: that man is responsible for all life around him. God didn't give man the right to exploit and abuse life, but rather he entrusted life into man's hands. All the birds and the beasts of creation, and also the grasses and trees and all the flora—*these* elements, as well as man's union with the rest of nature, with the universe, calls today for just as great a readjustment as the Church had to admit when the world was finally pronounced to be round. The Church was then committed to a flat world, and in the same way now, I think that some of the dogma stands in the way of this acceptance of the wonderful, spiritual qualities of the Bible and of the Church's teachings.

MCCULLOCH But you think that the young, for all their bizarre attempts, are after the right thing?

MENUHIN Absolutely. I think their instinct is right. What they reject—though they haven't yet learned to separate, shall we say, the wheat from the chaff—but what they reject is a good sign of what they are looking for, which is the responsibility of man to the rest of creation. If they keep looking for the other criteria instead of *only* commercial ones or only the crudest kind of survival in the immediate present, that, I think, all points to the fact that they are about to evolve and crystallize a new religious and a moral and a spiritual code, although, in many ways, this will only be the repetition of the truths already spoken by Jesus and by Buddha and by other great prophets. I am sure they are on the right track.

MCCULLOCH Do you see man at the moment as having as his chief sin, a kind of clumsiness?

MENUHIN Yes. I have always felt that his sins were really clumsiness, ignorance, stupidity, rather than vast and wonderful and exalted sins, you know, that deserve edifices and statues.

MCCULLOCH I have never heard that better put! You mean, as a certain parson once said, 'None of the people in my parish has scarlet sins, they are all dull brown'.

I see us blundering about in the most astonishing universe, in a kind of arrogant, silly way, like small children who don't know that things are beautiful, even. And I feel we have no real reverence for life.

MENUHIN Exactly. Man should behave with the utmost discretion. He is learning now, at great cost to himself and to the future, that in disturbing one little species—bacteria, or whatever it may be—he has often pulled down the whole edifice, the ecological balance of a particular area. And now what is happening, for instance, with the coral in the Pacific and other parts of the world, is appalling.

We are all becoming more aware of the complexity and interrelationship of everything, but our normal basis of operation is usually reduced to some far too simple criterion. If, for instance, we enter into a business deal, we merely think in terms of profit and loss. We must realize, let us say in prospecting for oil in Alaska, that the immediate profit from the oil, the immediate convenience and prosperity—that these are not sufficient. The future of the race, of humanity and of all life is at stake, and that the future would be better assured today by renouncing the use of oil altogether and going through a bad patch of a few years—say ten or fifteen years—until we have evolved some form of power and locomotion which would be absolutely compatible with life. There are plenty of such forms that exist: electricity, steam, earth heat generated from the centre of the earth, the sun, the winds, the tides. There is plenty of power about but we are led by habit like some stupid creature that has been conditioned to one reaction, a sort of Pavlov reflex. I am just giving this as an example. Man should move with great caution before he upsets any more applecarts. As you say, clumsiness is one of the chief sins.

MCCULLOCH I suppose this is what that very wise statement, 'Fools rush in where angels fear to tread', really means. I think man, at the moment, is the fool of the universe, would you agree?

MENUHIN Yes, very much so. But I would like to clear woman of some of the sins of man. I think spirituality, for instance, is something that is inherent and basic to women because they live it, they have their duty, their family, their children, and there is very little that escapes their commonsense, which includes a feeling for the future and the past. Man has to justify his existence because actually, in truth, he is disposable for the most part. He has to justify himself by creating, or making believe he creates, great things or memorable events. And sometimes he does: sculpture, architecture, music, compositions, drama, poetry, man has done extraordinary things and beautiful things in the past, but he is a dangerous animal because he will often try to over-justify his existence. I think he should just accept the fact that he is sometimes not really necessary, and be modest about it.

McCULLOCH I think you have omitted that woman's function is to tame man, domesticate him, and she hasn't quite succeeded.

MENUHIN No, unfortunately.

McCULLOCH One last question: How do you think we can restore man's faith in his own spiritual nature?

MENUHIN I think it is there already. All he has to be taught, is to open his eyes and become aware of it. And most people *are* aware of it, only not sufficiently so, and discipline of that awareness and the translation of that awareness into actual behaviour, is not sufficiently made clear. I think this is certainly one of the *cardinal* things which has been overlooked in educating the young. But when people come here, when they are moved by a great performance in music, by a Beethoven quartet or Bartok, or when they sit in a wonderful church or a cathedral, they are moved by these things. They know it when they read poetry or remember great lines of poetry, as most people have done in England, even those who are not formally educated. I remember hearing the most beautiful English spoken way up north, by a railway porter who—many years ago, that was—may not ever have gone to school but who knew it all from the Bible and their lovely way of speaking. These people are aware of it and it is not necessarily through the Ministry of Education. We are being educated all the time. Unfortunately many of the things we have to fill our minds with when we watch television or read most of the cheaper newspapers are not going to contribute to our mental climate. Many of the things that surround us are degrading. I think that censorship obviously isn't the answer, but a certain awareness in education would be the answer.

19 September 1970

I suppose that, at certain times, Margaret Drabble like lesser mortals must feel tired. But I have never heard her confess to it, not even when I visited her once in hospital. Her very pleasant face still wore its habitual expression of alert interest in all that was happening round her, and especially the people. Like several other women now in their mid-thirties she seems to be endowed with an unusually large share of creative energy. Celebrated as one of the very best of contemporary novelists, she is also a dutiful and devoted mother of three children, a learned lecturer of students, and fits into these activities an occasional appearance on the stage. Somehow, *mirabile dictu*, she has also found the time to give several first-class dialogues at St Mary-le-Bow.

The Drabble family has always bristled with brains as well as creative energy. Perhaps that is why Margaret does not seem to regard herself as particularly remarkable. As one might expect, she is a positive sort of person, who knows her own mind, but without ever being self-opinionated or didactic. Her habit of mind is reflective, so that in considering what others have to say, she is also exploring at a deeper level why they say it. What makes talking with her so interesting and enjoyable is that she genuinely prefers discussion to argument—in fact, she is an ideal dialoguer.

Berdyaev declared that God creates the world by imagination. To write a good or a great novel requires not only the ability to use language skilfully but also something of that divine power to give to airy nothing a a local habitation and a name, to breathe on the waters and confer a form of substantial life upon creatures who, till then, had neither form nor substance. Margaret would probably refuse an imputation of anything divine in her craft of novel-writing, and would be content to say that what she writes comes out of her own experience of the human situation and her reflection on it.

But to me the power of imagining creatively seems the most mysterious of all Pandora's gifts.

DIALOGUE WITH

Margaret Drabble

McCULLOCH I think, if I were pressed to say what Margaret Drabble is, I would say just that she was a born writer and that is a wonderful thing to be. There are an awful lot of people writing at the moment and I wish I could be convinced that many of them were born writers, but I *am* convinced that Margaret Drabble is—so I want to dive in at once.

The thing that interests me a great deal in modern novels—the really good ones anyhow—is how much more introspective they are. This is important, I think. Novels—good novels—reflect the age in which they are written. Do you think this is an age in which we are worried about ourselves? More than usual?

DRABBLE I think that people have been worried about themselves in every age but they have expressed it in different ways. I think you are quite right that nowadays we are introspective, and there are various reasons for this. We have become analytical as a result of discoveries about psychoanalysis and so on, and so we think about ourselves more, perhaps, than we used to and perhaps we have more time to think in. And the novel is certainly an excellent medium for describing one's thoughts about oneself, and for discussing internal processes. You can't do it so well on the stage because people have to be doing and speaking. In the novel you have time to look within and to discuss, for instance, what motivated somebody to do something, and you can peel away the layers. One is trying to discover the truth, the truth of the self; the meaning of life; why we are what we are and how we came to be so and whether it was an accident or not. These are the themes that one can explore.

McCULLOCH And you do it magnificently. But, even so, I want to know *why*, as usual. Do you think that there is more fear of life itself than there was?

DRABBLE Fear of life? I think there is a great deal more perplexity about life, because so many certainties have been taken away, so there is a great area of anxiety and uncertainty. I don't know about fear. I find a lot of modern life very frightening, but it is not the complicated things. The things I'm frightened of are technological things like aeroplanes and telephones, both of which frighten me very much. But one doesn't spend one's novels discussing that sort of fear. On the other hand, perhaps a massive wave of neurosis is indeed enveloping us because of fear of technology.

McCULLOCH Now, this is interesting because I would say that most of the people who come to see me are frightened of life, of the very fact of existence. That is very introspective, isn't it?

DRABBLE It is, but then, I think one would expect those to be the people who would come to one for help. I mean, a lot of people have good reason to be frightened of the things that life has done to them, and can do to them.

McCULLOCH But life has always been the same for this curious species, hasn't it? On this planet?

DRABBLE I wonder if it has. This is something I think about a lot, whether in fact, the nature and quality of human life has changed very greatly even in the last hundred years or so. I think, in certain respects, it probably has, that people's expectations and people's actual daily life are very different from what they were.

McCULLOCH You see, you mention machines. Well, I hate machines! I am pre-wheel, so my friends tell me.

DRABBLE Me too!

McCULLOCH We're together on that, then. But do you think that in the immense effort man has made to become technologically so clever, making these machines and so on, he has neglected faculties which are deeply important—inner faculties? Because your novels seem to me to beg that question.

DRABBLE I think—yes, quite certainly we have neglected inner faculties and a lot of us feel driven along at a pace we don't much like by the technological world we live in. But when you say one has neglected one's inner life, I think what you are really saying is, that I *over*-concentrate on the inner life?

McCULLOCH Well, I wouldn't criticize you to that extent because I don't think it is fair. I *do* know that you, in writing, reflect this concentration which is typical of the modern age. People are more aware of themselves than they ever were, I think.

DRABBLE Yes, I think they are, and there are a lot of reasons for this. You only have to open the newspaper and you find some scientific discussion of what the brain is, and this kind of thing, so naturally we all look into ourselves and wonder what we are. There used to be explanations for these things which were later proved in some cases to be false, and people feel very confused.

McCULLOCH You have now trailed a coat! You said, 'There used to be explanations' of, for instance, why we are here and what we are? Are you suggesting that my lot—the Church, I mean—have offered explanations that are not true?

DRABBLE No, I am not actually suggesting anything as daring as that. I think that people's ideas of why they were here used to be very simple and, for instance—what about the idea of heaven? People used to believe in that quite confidently, or at least they said they did. They don't now, and they are much more aware of man as a material being, because we've discovered far more about man, physically. I agree with you that this has probably been at the expense of understanding the spirit.

McCULLOCH Yes. You see, I think that the Church, early on, thought of man as a three-fold being: physical, mental and spiritual. We know a great deal nowadays about the relationship between the psyche and the physical. We still know very little about the spiritual.

DRABBLE Well, this is partly what I was trying to say when I said that we know more about ourselves. For instance, a hundred years ago it probably wouldn't have occurred to people, when they felt ill, to say, 'Am I ill because I am unhappy, or unhappy because I am ill?' Now everybody asks themselves that kind of question. It is sort of common thinking. Am I feeling ill because I don't want to go to work? Is my child ill because he doesn't want to go to school, or is he really ill? And I think we have become very conscious of this mental-physical overlap, and naturally we think about it a lot because it is interesting. But I quite agree that the deep spiritual forces that are motivating these connections—well, you say that very little is known about them. I certainly know very little about them.

McCULLOCH You see, obviously I am bound, because I am paid by an institution, to talk about these things, and I am fascinated by them, and so are you. So are we all. But it is just a great X.

I had to get vaccinated recently, to go abroad, and I went into my doctor's surgery and saw the usual sight—almost as full as this church—perhaps for the same reason! And I said to my nice G.P., 'Are they all ill?' and he said, 'Five per cent'. I said, 'And the rest?' He said, 'Well, they think they are ill, therefore they are ill'. Now isn't this what your books are about?

DRABBLE Absolutely, yes. I find this a very interesting problem. I agree that if you think you are ill, you often *are*, in a sense. Obviously, if you get so worried that you go and sit in a doctor's waiting-room, there *is* something wrong with you. This is exactly what you are saying—that we don't any longer know confidently whether it is our body, our mind or our spirit, because we know they are all mixed up together.

McCULLOCH Most people want attention, don't they?

DRABBLE They certainly want attention, and they go to the doctor to get it because no one else is giving it to them, maybe. They want somebody to be interested in them; you can see this every day with children. If they are terribly busy playing and they fall over and cut themselves, they don't stop, they just carry on bleeding and playing. But if they are fed up and cross, they make a tremendous drama out of a very small injury, because what they want is somebody to love them and pay attention and say they are terribly sorry. I think we all need attention because we cannot live without it. We are born, we come into the world helpless and crying, and unless immediate attention is paid we are going to peg out within twenty-four hours, or less.

McCULLOCH But the first few years of our life we are given, what I would call, unconditional attention, aren't we? Nothing is required of us; we just are looked after.

DRABBLE Should we be lucky enough to be born into a good home, yes. I think children need this and it is a natural thing to give it. The problems arise when adults go on behaving like children. I think one of the things that we have to teach our children is to pay attention to us in return, which is one of the ways of teaching them to grow up. There comes a point when a child is old enough to grasp the fact that one is terribly tired or that something frightful has happened, and they have just got to be good for a bit. That is the point at which they begin to pay attention back again.

I think, in a good relationship between parents and children there is always attention, but it becomes two-way instead of only one-way. In fact, it becomes two-way very quickly, if one thinks about it, because a little baby will begin to smile, and realizes that it is giving pleasure by smiling. It isn't simply wailing all the time.

McCULLOCH Now, do you find that there is any parallel between all this and man's relation to the universe? I don't want to be theological but between us and the background—you know, behind it all—there is a desire to be convinced that this kind of love is still operative. I have to deal with people of all ages and they all seem to me to be asking the assurance of that particular love that you gave your children at the very beginning. People *want* this. Now *I* think—why should I pester you with what I think? But I see people today deprived of something that was there before—though you say it is all baloney now—you know, the conviction that behind the whole damn thing there is a loving purpose; that not a sparrow falls to the ground, and so on.

DRABBLE Yes, I think people did feel that and I think they find it increasingly difficult to believe it now, in view of the horrific evidence around them.

McCULLOCH Was the evidence so different then? I mean, you could be a Christian in the days of Genghis Khan, couldn't you?

DRABBLE Yes, you could, though you probably did not know quite as much about Genghis Khan as we know about various disasters going on at this moment. I think that probably we are more aware of the relentless nature of violence in the world than people used to be, because they led more isolated lives.

McCULLOCH I wonder. Because nothing could be more unpleasant, I imagine, than a horde of Visigoths coming through the village.

DRABBLE Yes, but I can't help feeling that when the horde of Visigoths came through the village, people's faith in Divine Love was shaken. They probably thought that something had gone wrong with their God, and doubted for a while. I certainly would.

McCULLOCH Do you think people are introspective and lonely in the face of life because they just haven't any idea of God?

DRABBLE I think so, yes. But you could put it in less theological terms by saying, that they have no idea of the meaning of their existence, and indeed they haven't. And I am sure that in the next hundred years, discoveries are going to be made that will confuse us even more about our role on earth and the course of evolution. I think people are quite right to be confused and anxious.

McCulloch Wait a moment. I must have that again, it is very interesting. You say that in the next hundred years people will know more about the role of man on earth?

Drabble Yes, and they may well become even more depressed about it.

McCulloch But don't you believe that there may be a tremendous return of man as a religious animal? I mean, he is going through a phase now of being frightfully self-concerned and egotistic, but won't it result duly in the very opposite, that he will realize that he relies upon what is behind the universe?

Drabble Yes, indeed. I think there are signs of this now. There are religious movements, there is a need for the spiritual which sometimes expresses itself in rather strange ways. But what bothers me is, is this need going to be met? In other words, is God actually there? That is what I am worried about. I feel the need for God but I think that he might not feel any need for me any more. One might need and seek and never find.

McCulloch The only way to search for God is in humility.

Drabble I think that one couldn't say that everybody who searched in humility, found. I feel rather depressed about this at the moment.

McCulloch Pretty certainly, I think. Anybody who sits in front of the wonder of existence in the right attitude will find God all right. You don't think so?

Drabble I would like to think so, that is as far as I am prepared to commit myself.

McCulloch That, I think, is the best modern statement I have ever heard. You know, I once saw a thing in a Sunday paper, on 'The God I Would Like'—you know, elected by popular ballot. Now, if God is God you don't go about it like that.

Drabble Yes, but this is rather like the sort of game that children play at school: 'If I hadn't had my mother, I would rather have so-and-so for my mother'. They discuss which is the best mother and that kind of thing. And I agree you don't go about it like that. You've got the one you've got. But I think one is rather ignoring the facts when one says that all mothers are good mothers; some mothers aren't good. Can you presuppose, from the *need* for a good mother, or the need for love and attention, that somebody will supply it?

McCULLOCH I simply say that I think the *kind* of love which mothers give—though if prolonged, it would be very dangerous and would inhibit growth of personality, which I think God is after—I do say that that kind of love reflects the nature of the love behind the universe.

DRABBLE I would like to think that this was so, because I do feel, about my own feeling for my children, that it is a very pure and instinctive and unquestioned thing. On the other hand, I can't have the same confidence in God as a father as I have in myself as a mother, which is a terrible thing to say.

McCULLOCH You see, all we worry about, in my trade, you know, is that people should realize that behind life is a love infinitely more real than the parental love they have met. Forget about father, mother, or anything else. I have only used the analogy of mother-love because it is utterly unconditional. If we can live our lives firmly convinced that behind the mess we are making of things, there is the kind of love that the mother shows her new-born babe, then, I think—you may say you are cheating yourself—but I have come to the conclusion that it is the most reasonable explanation of existence that there is.

DRABBLE I think it is reasonable but then I haven't had it disproved to me and I am a naturally cheerful and optimistic person. But I do find it rather hard to convince other people who have much better arguments to back them up. In the end, all they say to me is, 'All you mean is that you *feel* that God exists', and I say, 'Yes, quite right, I *do* feel it'.

McCULLOCH Well, here we are, flung on to this planet, we don't know what the heck we are here for and yet, is it conceivable that the best thing we know isn't the ultimate thing behind the whole universe? And I think love is the best thing we have ever known. Now, it is a fair question.

DRABBLE It is a very fair question, and I agree it *is* almost inconceivable that the phenomenon of man should have been a pure kind of fluke in the universe, as various people are trying to persuade us. I think it is almost impossible that consciousness could be a mistake of evolution and that the craving and need for spiritual knowledge or love should be unanswered. I think it *could* be possible; I simply can't quite believe that it is.

McCULLOCH You don't think Jesus might be right when he said, why are you so frightened of life? You know—why have you got so little faith? Because within a few seconds you could change the whole thing and stop hating each other, stop being frightened of each other and so on.

DRABBLE Of course one could, but people don't, do they?

MCCULLOCH I think Jesus may yet come into his own. I don't see anybody else who can.

DRABBLE There is no alternative, I agree with you there.

12 September 1972

It was a particularly gracious act of Sir Laurence Olivier (as he was then) to do a dialogue for us, when he was convalescing after a severe illness, and was also at an important stage in his great task of raising the National Theatre on the South Bank; though he did say that the reintroduction of the earliest form of drama into the Church seemed to him well worthy of support. He and Lady Olivier were held up in a traffic jam and the delay meant that there was little time before the dialogue to map out what we would discuss. But, because a great deal of the value of these weekly conversations lies in the fact that they are impromptu, this occasion was, if anything, all the more fascinating for that.

His High Church parson father was renowned as a preacher, one of the spell-binders more frequent in the pulpits of yesteryear than today. Laurence Olivier, on arriving in the pulpit of St Mary-le-Bow, was undoubtedly spell-binding, but clearly had no intention of emulating his father's pulpit style. He leaned on the tasselled cushion, and drew the crowded audience into an atmosphere of friendly informality, talking almost diffidently about his life and work. What most impressed us all was the simplicity and unaffectedness of his manner.

I think that many of the City audience had been expecting that this world-famous actor, whom they had seen in many commanding roles, would dominate the building with his great personality. It was, however, an off-stage performance he gave us, offering his views and thoughts almost apologetically, as though he hesitated to inflict his opinions on his hearers.

I suppose that all really great acting requires, before all else, a kind of self-emptying, a willingness to give up your own prejudices and self-assertion in order to enter by imagination into the role you are given to interpret. I am sure on the occasion of Lord Olivier's dialogue many of us came to this understanding, perhaps for the first time.

DIALOGUE WITH

Laurence Olivier

McCULLOCH At the outset, I want—if you will give it—some idea of the vision behind, what I suppose is the most exciting thing that is happening at the moment, the vision of the National Theatre. What is it going to *do*?

OLIVIER Well, I think that question provides me with a sort of 'can't-see-the-wood-for-the-trees' escape! What is it going to do? It is awfully difficult for me to see anything beyond the fact that it is going to *be*—if it is. I suppose it isn't bang certain yet. None of us has broken open the bottle of champagne yet. We are not going to do it until the first earth is turned over, and that won't be till next summer. When *that*—it sounds funny and the wrong way round—but when that has started, I suppose one has to think what it is going to *be*.

Now the vision, I'm afraid, stops rather short of what you would hope it might. It will get bigger, and other, far better men than I will invent it, create it, and stagger forward with it. I have wanted there to be a National Theatre and now, at this very moment, having been faced with this question, I have got to ask myself, 'Why?'

I believe in the theatre. I believe that the art of the actor is important for the life of the people, that they may study the art of the actor, because through his art—and I think it *is* an art—I am not ducking that and calling it an interpretative craft—it can teach the human heart the knowledge of itself. And I think, never has an age required that more than this age does.

When it was first presented—I suppose in the English theatre in Elizabethan times—I daresay it was an essential then. It certainly burst upon us at that time, the *power* of dramatic thought and the fact that only through the art of acting can such thought be conveyed, and so I think, it is natural for us to want to promulgate it.

When I go North, I am asked, 'Why London; why not Glasgow?' Well, I think that answers itself really. It isn't as snobbish as all that to start in London, it *is* the capital of our country, and it is the largest city, I believe, in the world. A lot of things start in London. And therefrom we may travel—through a process of jealousy perhaps—into other towns. There is, after all, a certain amount of vying, of rivalry, between towns such as Coventry and Birmingham. If one town has a building of thirty storeys, you may be sure the other town is going to have it within a very few weeks. Therefore, if London has a National Theatre, if the centre of the country's interest in theatre is in London, that itch would then exist and we hope, to a degree which will cause people with that itch to create the same thing in other towns. In other words, what we are roughly going towards, I would say, as a first essay in the subject, are probably Civic Theatres. I don't think the Government is going to be able to undertake theatres in every town and therefore the local government in every town must do it for themselves, if they so wish. And so long as we, at the National Theatre, keep our standard, or create our standard and make of it something enviable enough in London, then in Manchester, if they really get angry enough and if they really care about it, they will have to do the same thing there. In that way the thing will flow around. That is the only way that I can see that this particular tide of this particular tiny little gulf-stream, can work.

McCULLOCH And how do you think the great god Money will look on this?

OLIVIER Well, I think in our case, the Government has kept faith with us.

McCULLOCH I like that, because I said the great god Money and you said the Government!

OLIVIER I meant that the Government had kept faith with us in not being too impressed by the great god Money. May I put it like that? The Greater London Council has also kept faith with us pretty well all right. We have had, in order to arrive at the sum proposed now, to cut down on our requirements to a considerable extent. From my point of view, if I may refer to the artistic side, we have, initially, to do without one of the little gems in our plan, which was to be the experimental theatre. Space for this will still be incorporated in the building, but it will not be equipped, not at first anyway, and not unless prices keep down, which is most unlikely, and unless economies can possibly be made, which is equally unlikely.

McCULLOCH Can we get off money, because I feel it is not your subject nor is it mine? I see the vision of a man coming to London, like one going to ancient Athens, and being certain of seeing a great play before he left. Is that right?

OLIVIER You could say that. It is not always guaranteed to be a *great* play. I always judge an evening or an afternoon in the theatre as a show. If it a great play—marvellous! I am very lucky because one gets written about every ten years, but you need an awful lot more plays than that. If you do find a great play you are very lucky, as I say. If you don't, then at least you must find remarkable performances or team-work in it, or a remarkable star-performance or a wonderful production and presentation; the perfect treatment given to whatever kind of play it is. At least you must have *that*. I certainly don't demand, as some of our critics, I think, do, a great *play*, I demand a marvellous show. And by that, I don't mean a show in its usual, frivolous sense. I want a great show. For instance, nobody in the world has ever claimed that Richard III is a great play, but if they see some fellow up there really giving it the works, he has had a decent enough afternoon and he should not ask for his money back.

McCULLOCH Now, this is something that has always puzzled me: is great acting more important than a great play?

OLIVIER I don't think any play can live very healthily without at least very good acting. On the other hand, one can see certain plays by extremely inexperienced casts, and be moved by them. I have been terribly touched—I remember, years ago, going to the George Inn Churchyard the other side of the River, on Shakespeare's birthday and seeing—I beg your pardon, George Inn *Yard*, not churchyard! I am so overwhelmed finding myself where I am! Yes, the *George Inn Yard*, where they used to act plays in the old days, possibly before the Globe Playhouse arrived, and I saw a performance of *Romeo and Juliet* there. It was only the Balcony Scene, and it was done by amateurs, a young chap in a rather terrible costume from a rather terrible costumiers somewhere, and the girl—I think probably she had made her little white thing herself—and they did the Balcony Scene. Well, there was something about the extreme ingenuousness of the afternoon that was extremely touching and it caused one to think that perhaps a thing as great as the Balcony Scene in *Romeo and Juliet* is all right in anybody's hands, but I think that rather depends upon the alchemy that surrounds it. If they, the young people, are at least terribly sincere, if they throw their souls into it, then it will be touching in spite of the fact that it won't be exactly adept or skilful.

McCULLOCH Now this is interesting to me personally, because the best Andrew Aguecheek I ever saw was a thirteen year old boy. I suppose at the age of thirteen you can play a fool. Now I am interested to know why this is true, if it is true. Can a young actor, for instance, play Hamlet?

OLIVIER Yes, I have seen very good Hamlets: I saw Alec Guinness play it when he was twenty-three, extraordinarily good, obviously not technically equipped to the extent desirable to play a huge part like that—he would shout a bit, scream, fall into the usual young actor's faults, exhaust himself in certain scenes and that sort of thing. His technical skill wasn't anything like what it is today. He is one of the most skilful actors we have ever had, I should think.

McCULLOCH This brings me to the mystery of the whole thing. There is a mystery behind it, I hope you will agree? What I am interested to discover is this: I have never been an actor, but in a sense *everybody* is an actor—I mean, to the extent that they all put on masks and try to be what they think people will most admire. There is always this mystery behind human personality. Now, does an actor go home for his supper after acting Hamlet, say, quite the same chap?

OLIVIER No, I think the experience of going through an ordeal like that would have the same bearing on a person as going through any painful ordeal. Hamlet is not what I would call a particularly punishing role, it is hard, very hard work, and emotionally quite tough. Plays are always tough if they finish with a fight, because you add to emotional and mental exhaustion, physical exhaustion as well. So you do a splendid act of puffing when you go in front of the curtain to take your bow. But Hamlet is not by any means the most punishing role. Macbeth is a dreadful experience to go through, Othello is an appalling experience, Titus Andronicus is a very rare experience but very, very tough indeed.

I don't think what our parents' generation thought of actors can be quite true. It used to be thought that the best actors were those who went through their performance simply wondering what they were going to have for supper, or what won the 3.30. Personally, I don't think that is true. I think that you have to feel, you *have* to feel, and if you go through an experience like King

Lear, or Titus Andronicus, you really have to make it real to the audience and to yourself. To go through the experience of actually acting, feeling these tremendous emotions—you can't just wave that aside. Therefore it does, of course, do something to you. We hope it slightly enlarges the soul; I don't know what it does.

MCCULLOCH Mrs Siddons, I am told, when she was doing her greatest roles, was mentally thinking of the household accounts. Do you think that is at all possible?

OLIVIER I don't think it is. She may have said so, and she may have been naughty once. We are all guilty of being naughty occasionally; we get bored—yes, I am sorry, it is possible. Perhaps something happens to make us have the giggles or something absolutely filthy like that, which is very wicked and never allowed at the National Theatre! Sometimes a thought might lead us astray and we might wonder whether Oxford or Cambridge were winning the Boat-race. It is possible but hardly probable in what I'd call a punishing role. I don't think you could dart off like that; you'd have to be wholly in it. Just like in a cell.

MCCULLOCH I am curiously interested in drama, simply because it sails so very close to my own job. But you can't put Christianity on the stage at all, can you? I suppose the trouble is, we have reduced it to a kind of moralism, while you are doing the great theological things: talking about the redemption of man and the grace of God and so on. There is terrific drama in Christianity but now if you try to put a parson on the stage it is a calamity, isn't it, on the whole?

OLIVIER I think, you know, the medium has shifted from the state of receptiveness in which you just accepted what people said. You can't really put on a political play and get nearer to the bones of the matter than gentle philosophy. I think that the nearest to a brilliant political exponent we have ever had in drama in the last fifty or sixty years, was Chekov, because his message is absolutely clear, and yet he never refers to the message at all. It's just that the behaviour of the people makes the message clear. *That* is the use of the theatre. I don't think the use is for people to get up and make a haranguing speech on the side of Chelsea Football team or something, and bring the house down with the success of the speech because they believe what he says is true. I don't think that is the object of the theatre.

My father—he was of your cloth, as you know—and he used to say that if I wasn't going to follow in his footsteps and be a priest, at least I was doing something, in the theatre, where I could be very useful preaching. It didn't quite work out like that. This is the nearest I have ever got to it.

McCULLOCH I cannot believe that your father, whom I met, was as Protestant as *that.* I don't think he was interested in your *preaching.*

The main question I want to ask you is, do you believe that 'All the world's a stage'? And if so, what is the play all about?

OLIVIER Shakespeare said it was, so I suppose what is good enough for him is good enough for you and me. Yes, it is. What is it all about? It's about strife, it's about torment, disappointment, love, sacrifice, humour, about golden sunsets and black storms; it's to a certain extent, about leadership, I suppose, though not nearly so much as it is about service. I think that as far as the human problem is concerned, it would be a help if people could regard themselves, willingly, as servants. I think if you can regard your life, and the object of it, simply in the light of the certainty that to serve is the best thing to do, then I think everybody could be reasonably happy, from the Queen down to the poorest washer of your toilet floor.

McCULLOCH But haven't you left out something which might be. . . .

OLIVIER I'm sure I have. Do tell me what it is.

McCULLOCH That, I think, is rather unfair of you! I was going to say, don't you think you have left something out about getting on with other people on the stage?

OLIVIER Yes, I think that is covered in the word 'service', isn't it? We believe in love, we're very fond of each other, we think that that is an essential part of running a company—that people get on very well. I think that our standards owe an awful lot to the idea that you can do more if you are helped to do it. And that doesn't mean in the least bit that everybody adulates everybody, or that nobody is critical of anybody. That isn't proper and certainly not true.

McCULLOCH I remember that Athene Seyler, a mutual friend, in that pulpit, when this thing came up, said that the funny thing about the world being a stage was, why did we come on it so unrehearsed? And she thought of death in that way too. She thought that she would arrive—at whatever there is to come—in a kind of unrehearsed state, and this worried her considerably.

Isn't this what this business is about—the Church throughout the ages?

OLIVIER You mean, to rehearse you? Yes. And it's typical of Athene to be so worried about it.

MCCULLOCH It's typical of her because she is the most common-sense person I've ever met. Now, this is very curious to me—it's my last question, I'm afraid—and it is this: the woman of this century—the 'new woman'—is a quite new sort of person with a highly developed consciousness, and yet there aren't many great women's parts being written by modern playwrights, are there? And I am curious to know why.

OLIVIER I think probably they are at this moment being written. One must remember that emancipation is happening at an extraordinary speed, though it may take a thousand years before the equation is finally solved between the sexes. I think a lot of patience is being used on all sides. Obviously, the sexes can get up against each other the way any two individuals can. I suppose there is good enough reason for that. It's very hard, the closeness, as we all know—talking real dog-stuff now—the blood and hate so close and the sympathy and antipathy so close.

MCCULLOCH Yes, I agree. Now, I thought one of the greatest dramatic roles you ever played, apart from Malvolio, was in *The Entertainer*, which was a kind of negative nobility, a might-have-been, and I thought it revealed more of human nature than I had seen on the stage for a very long time. Do you think I am right about that?

OLIVIER Well, you've touched on almost, I shall say, my very favourite role. I adored doing that more than anything. I did it for nearly forty weeks and I never, never got tired. There was something about it: the characterization was immensely shrewd and closely observed on the part of the author. He knew his man backwards and I just happened to find it very easily. Sometimes one does. I just smelt it out very easily and, almost first shot, managed to assume the right sort of characteristics, the right sort of appendages to characterization. It just worked out right and I loved doing it.

MCCULLOCH Is there any hope of getting it back? Because I think it's worth a thousand sermons.

OLIVIER I don't know.

May I just say one thing? I'm always going on, blinding on

about the theatre, and people look at me as if I were insane, because there *are* other things. There is something called the movies and I am told there is something called the telly, but what I mean by the theatre as against those two is this: that the nature of a live audience to a live person acting for them, is quite different from that which addresses itself to a screen upon which are thrown shapes by light through celluloid, or upon some mechanism which I can't even begin to understand, called 'the box'. In the theatre, you are not too far away from me and I'm not too far away from you, to see any expression on your face, and that is right. That relationship, that experience, is to me, and to those who like the theatre better than they like other forms of entertainment, to people, rare birds such as us, that experience is a keener one than those offered by the reproductive processes.

I know, of course, I am biased, but I think that the experience of seeing wonderful acting on the stage, wonderful scenes played, marvellous moments, being caught up in a drama and seeing things go on and thinking, 'It's true, it's true!' and all of those truths hammering home, so that you go away afterwards a little bit richer—I think that is one of the *great* experiences, and I want our country to have that all over the place.

That is why we're starting the National, so that they will have it here. And perhaps better men than I will appear on the horizon to guide them towards it.

8 October 1968

As she came into the church, the crowded audience erupted into a spontaneous applause of welcome. If ever there was anyone with whom they felt in personal *rapport*, it was certainly she, the communicator *par excellence*. Whether the people with her are two or three gathered together, or thousands, or indeed millions, she is the same radiant person, spontaneous, free, aware and very much alive, exceptionally gifted and utterly sincere, serious and humorous, swift in sympathy, a brilliant mimic and comedienne; above all, a fundamentally happy woman. What she communicates in any medium is an unusual understanding of our common humanity, completely devoid of malice and all uncharitableness. Joyce Grenfell can expose our comic crassness—and yet more our tragic stupidity, and leave us somehow feeling that behind it all the universe is not against us.

To describe her professionally merely as an actress is a considerable understatement. She is chiefly famous as a *diseuse*, writing all her own material for her character sketches and songs. One of the happiest evenings at the theatre or on television is when Joyce is the sole performer, and you are taken through an enchanting variety of her adroit impressions of characters both comic and pathetic, magically peopling the stage with *dramatis personae* who exist only in her imagination and yours. Tall, commanding in stage presence, graceful in movement, she can yet become a waif, a duchess, a harassed school-teacher, what you will.

Her personal friends know her as one who enjoys a happy married life, not far off its golden anniversary, and as a phenomenally hard worker who still has time to give to others her hospitality and to share theirs. Basically she is serious-minded, as her published writings often reveal. It is because she sees that life for many people is a hard grind that she has worked to lighten it with her gift of laughter.

DIALOGUE WITH

Joyce Grenfell

McCulloch I think, Joyce, you are without doubt a person who is extraordinarily alive, and I thought we might talk today about 'being alive'—what *makes* people alive. Are you agreed? It's a large question I'm afraid!

Grenfell Well, for me, I think it is expressing what I understand God to be. If you ask, 'What is Life?', I suppose life is the presence of God. I think that people are lively—I don't mean in a euphoric, hysterical way, but in the sense of being aware—because they are more conscious of that which truly *is*.

I remember years ago being invited to do a part in a series on radio. *Wishes for a Godchild* was the subject, and I began to think about it and found that the thing I would wish for anybody I loved would be the possibility of never coming to the end of discovery. I think it is what makes life worth living. I think what one wants to discover is what life is for, what is real, what you can depend on, what never changes, and that you yourself should be changeable enough to let go of the things that have no real value. Mark you, I didn't do that when I was very young.

McCulloch Were you looking for Joyce Grenfell?

Grenfell No, I don't think so. I think I knew her! No, actually, I think what I was doing, what I am doing now, is *losing* Joyce Grenfell, or hoping to, and finding out—this sounds very solemn, but I think this is the right place to say it—finding out the person God made. The older you get the more you realize that happiness is losing your false sense of what you are, your *false self*. What was that lovely quotation you told me upstairs just now? Goethe, was it?

McCulloch 'Become what you are.'

Grenfell 'Become what you are.' Well that, interpreted, means become what your true potential is, your true spiritual wholeness.

McCulloch I think it means that God knows what we essentially are and we have got to realise it ourselves.

Grenfell Yes. Going back to what we were saying about 'living' and 'being alive', I don't know if you remember the 'Face to Face' programme that Lord Reith did with John Freeman many years ago? I remember at the very end Freeman said to him, 'Do you have any regrets?' and he lifted that great granite head and he said, 'Yes, for discovering too late that life is for living', and I thought, with a sense of compassion that living is *being*, and it isn't just *living it up* or *getting out there and doing more*. That is part of it, I think, but living, as I see it, is learning to *be*.

McCulloch Joyce, have you ever looked up the phrase 'dear me'? It's worth doing one day, in Brewer's. 'Dear me' is a very curious phrase which is in practically every language. The Germans say, 'Ach du liebe Zeit'. In other words, 'Ah, my beloved spirit'.

Grenfell 'Dear me'—of course, it must mean 'dear *real* me'. One of the things people want to do today is to be themselves all the time, which usually doesn't mean anything except being disobedient. The young say, 'Well, I just must be myself'. But until you find out what your real self is, you can't be it, can you?

McCulloch I saw you once with a lot of young people. It was one of those rare occasions when I have seen somebody coping with them properly on a telly programme.

Grenfell Well, I don't think I was conscious of *coping*. We were communicating, we were getting on and making real contact.

But to get back to this 'me' for a moment. So many people say, almost unconsciously with a sort of pride, 'Well, I'm afraid I've got a terribly short temper. It's just the way I am', or, 'I'm just one of those people, I can't help it'. But really they *can*. They *are* capable of change, of changing to that which is changeless.

McCulloch The other day I got a letter from somebody I had tried to help for a long, long time, and it said at the end, 'I'm sorry I'm such a mess'.

Grenfell Yes. Well there is a bit of pride in that, isn't there? It's being individual in the wrong sense of individual. But talking about living and being alive, it is rather interesting to look at the people that you find attractive in life. What are the qualities that have drawn you to them, the lively people? Very often, they are certain qualities of the spirit like honesty, courage, generosity, selflessness, and I would put quite high up, enthusiasm. If you look up 'enthusiasm' in a dictionary, it says 'possessed by a god'. Well, I would drop the 'a'. I think real enthusiasm is being possessed by God or, in other words, responding to something that is, in fact, eternal, and is the thing that gives you a sense of confidence.

McCULLOCH There are certain people, are there not, who make others more alive?

GRENFELL Yes, or who draw out that which is already there. I have discovered this about audiences, that you can only get out of them what is already there. If you take that to be a total potential, and assume that man is an intelligent creature that he has got a sense of humour, you will find it. This life-enhancing is a kind of sharing, really.

McCULLOCH I suppose that when you do really communicate with somebody else, there is always a come-back, a reciprocity.

GRENFELL Yes, and Joseph, hasn't this got a lot to do with happiness? Because being alive is, in a sense, a happy state to be in, or a state of fulfilment. Have you noticed that when you are truly happy you are never aware of yourself? Never. And in fact if you say, 'Oh my goodness, I am happy at this moment', it's gone. You should never stop and say, 'Today I feel so happy, happy, happy'. Very depressing!

McCULLOCH But it is fairly obvious that an enormous proportion of the world's population are not very much alive. One has to face the fact that there are certain people—and it is the minority—who have this quality of aliveness and are doing the job of kindling the others, apparently.

GRENFELL What do you think *is* the most important job to do? Isn't it to make people more aware of their own potential? I go round to schools quite a lot and it seems to me we do the most marvellous job with our children up to the age of about eleven. The liveliness, the awareness of the children, and somehow the dedication of the teaching of the early years are really exciting. Yet, when they get to the age of about eleven and they go to the bigger schools and have to get down to, what I suppose you would call, hard work, the magic goes out of it. Isn't it odd! But if you look back at your own life and all the examples that have influenced you, nearly always there was somebody at school who, in fact, sparked off something for you. The question is, how do we retain this longing to share what has sparked us off with other people?

McCULLOCH Indeed, yes! But what about the difficulty of getting out of the cradle to start with? I mean the persistent idea, which is an infantile one, that we are the centre of the universe? A lot of us in middle age and even older still seem convinced that the centre of the universe is number one.

GRENFELL That, I think, is why we are unhappy, because this being 'alive' is simply becoming aware that 'I' *includes* it all. It is a really basic, very simple thing and it has, oddly enough, got nothing to do with circumstances, has it? The moment of light is when you realize that you contain the universe; when you cease to be the important little me, and become part of the whole.

McCULLOCH Would you say that a child was more alive than most of the grown-up people around him?

GRENFELL Yes, in an unconscious way. I remember once sitting in a garden in Northumberland and the daughter of a great friend of mine—she was about three—picked a daisy in that rather cruel way children pick flowers, without a stem, just a head. She put it on my knee and said—and I will try to quote this accurately—she said, 'When I are asleep. I don't know nothing of me'. That, together with the flower put on my knee, was an experience I would never like to forget.

McCULLOCH I once saw you, in one of your stage sketches, take a class of children. Not one of them was visible and yet we all saw them. That must have been because of the way you yourself perceived them. Now, is perception a great deal to do with being alive?

GRENFELL I think it is. But I have come to the conclusion that 'discernment' is a better word than 'perception'. It is the next step, isn't it? First you perceive, then you discern. I am being much more solemn than you today, aren't I? But I find it very interesting. We were talking about Blake just now upstairs, and that marvellous quotation which we neither of us got right, so we had to look it up:

To see a world in a grain of sand
And a heaven in a wild flower,
Hold infinity in the palm of your hand
And eternity in an hour.

He really knew everything, Blake.

That's being alive, down to earth and practical. I just wish that we could all be aware of what there is to see and discover in the world, like flowers and birds and buildings and people's faces. It all belongs to us *all*, that is the thing. It isn't my peculiar privilege to know the difference between a tree-creeper and a nuthatch. I mean you can do it too.

McCULLOCH I'm afraid I *don't* know the difference! You sound exactly like my wife. She says that it is awfully important to know that a tulip is a tulip and a rose is a rose and so on and that only if you give it that much attention do you really *see* it, or, as you would say, discern it.

GRENFELL I don't think it need have a name, but I think it is nice that you recognize it and salute it. It is there to see. It's so easy to be starry-eyed about nature and all that kind of thing. But we are going to have so much more leisure, and we have got to do something with it. The happy people I know are people with interests.

McCULLOCH What is it, in other people, that really interests *you*, Joyce?

GRENFELL When I was young, I just looked at people and most of them were funny. I found that I could reproduce the sounds they made and sometimes the faces—I have a face that makes all kinds of faces. Now I am much more interested in what people are really like and in finding the meeting-place, looking for what is real in them. I don't sit on buses and do this very consciously all the time, but this is basically what it is about.

McCULLOCH There's no doubt there is something in you which responds quickly to anybody else.

GRENFELL Yes. I have discovered in my life that if you are face to face with somebody, you can get on with that person, even if you don't like him. You find what is true and real about him, and that is the only thing that matters.

McCULLOCH A rather wonderful Jew said that 'real life is meeting'—would you agree with him?

GRENFELL Yes, I would go a long way with that. I don't think it's the whole thing but I think it is one of the steps.

McCULLOCH Joyce, may I ask you a very personal question? Have you ever met anybody who didn't respond? You know, upon whom your whole personality reacted like a pea off a tank?

GRENFELL Obviously, yes. But in some sort of way you don't have to have a row about it. You stand your ground in your heart and you find that your paths diverge.

I remember during the war, my job was working in hospital wards, entertaining. Sometimes you would go into a ward and meet a man who did not want to be entertained and resented your presence. At first I was off-put by this. You would see them turn away from you—in fact, sometimes they picked up the newspaper and read it right in your face. It was terribly daunting. Then I started to think, 'But who the hell am *I*? Why *should* he like me, especially if I am going to react instantly to his animosity? If I can include him in some way. . . .' You see, you don't have to like a person, you only have to love him. And it very often worked, because he would put the paper down and look over his shoulder a bit, pretending he *wasn't* looking, and then sometimes he would turn completely and join in, and become part of the group. This was not—I must make this very clear—this was not my personality working on his personality. It was a wish to include, not to fence off. I think that is something I have found with people who aren't ready to respond; it is how *we* react to their indifference that matters.

MCCULLOCH Why do people get turned in on themselves like that? There is no doubt about Wordsworth's 'Shades of the prison-house begin to close upon the growing boy'. This does happen.

GRENFELL Yes. The tragedy is, the spontaneity of the child gets crushed. But there is far less reason actually, for this to happen in the world today, I think, than there was when I was a child. The problem today is that there is apparently so much freedom that people don't know where they are; they are dizzy with freedom.

MCCULLOCH That is a wonderful phrase, 'dizzy with freedom'. It's a very good description of our age.

GRENFELL Yes! I've never thought of it before. But, Joseph, the interesting thing is that we make our own prison walls, don't we? And young people who are against what they call 'convention' are in fact hemmed in by a whole barricade of conventions of their own devising—they look alike, dress alike, and think alike.

MCCULLOCH They are, in fact, equally imprisoned. I suppose that most of us are rather the types who find life a bit defeating. You know, there are so many people to be anxious about, and the present world is full of pressures that irritate and confine and shut us in on ourselves. And we are overcrowded, too. We know that outside our prison gates there is some vision, fresh air, freedom, but we can't reach it. I am being very deliberately depressing because it does seem somewhat the psychological state of the modern world.

I wonder if anyone knows the source of this quotation: 'What can sadden those who serve the everlasting joy?' That seems the clue to the whole thing, doesn't it. I'd like to know who said it.

GRENFELL Yes, I would, too. You said just now that we know that there is light and fresh air and everything out there, but we can't reach it. The discovery that seems essential to me is the discovery that the kingdom of heaven is within. What is the good, though, of knowing this unless you express it in some way which is a fulfilment of living?

McCULLOCH There was another great wit who said very much the same thing: 'What is the good of putting a lamp under a bed?'

GRENFELL Yes, that's right—bushel.

McCULLOCH No, but surely you have put your finger on it? That it is only people who can give out, express what is in them, that are going to be of use in this world and find the way to the abundant life.

GRENFELL This 'being of use', being responsible, is important. I heard something the other day which I liked enormously. It's semantics, it's playing with words but I did rather like it, because one of the qualities I find attractive in people is this sense of responsibility. Somebody said to me, 'Have you heard a rather nice description of what "responsibility" means? It's man's response to God's ability.' I find that rather nice.

McCULLOCH May I ask: is that close to what you mean by 'being alive'?

GRENFELL Yes, it is.

3 April 1973

Since Dr Arnold the image of the public school headmaster has undergone a number of transformations. The authoritarian 'beak' became the somewhat slick showman and salesman, who in turn became the brisk, business-like administrator. In the last two decades, however, they have done much better than that, certainly in those greater and renowned schools which set the pace and fashion for the others. The pseudo-Arnold skin has been sloughed, and to a large extent the élitist upper middle-class pretensions abandoned. Quiet, far from self-assertive men, dedicated to the ideal of shaping the public school to fulfil an essential role in a vastly changed social structure, were appointed headmasters. They wield no less authority, but of the kind which is based much more on love than on fear.

This new pattern of headmastership is admirably exemplified in Michael McCrum. He invited me to Tonbridge in the year before he was appointed to Eton, and I saw and admired then the way in which, without becoming part of the background, he refused to dominate the foreground, and conducted the school's affairs in easy and friendly relationship with both his colleagues and their pupils. To the outsider a school's life always seems a perpetual process of being summoned by bells and of running to keep up with the exigencies of the immediate situation. This is because the outsider, if his schooldays were long ago, remembers the inexorable time-table, and the feeling that your life was never your own. Under Michael McCrum's aegis, one felt that this situation had been effectively remedied, and that within the framework of the considerable amount of work which the modern syllabus demands of the pupil, there was far more personal freedom and psychological room than the old pattern allowed. I suspect that Michael McCrum would say that nobody can effectively educate until he himself has arrived there, though he would hasten to add that it is always a struggle to stay there.

DIALOGUE WITH

Michael McCrum

McCulloch Mr McCrum [the Headmaster of Eton] has one of the most difficult and most rewarding jobs in the modern world.

The young at the moment are slightly bewildered, to say the least—I suppose, because they've got more freedom of choice than any young have ever had. I can't help thinking that must also be a strain on those who have to educate them. Would that be true?

McCrum Yes, I think it is. I started from a slightly different background from many schoolmasters because I was a don at Cambridge for a good many years, and there you are used to discussing things without ever having to *do* anything about them, which is a very comfortable position to be in, whereas in a school you have to decide quite definitely one way or the other, give your views and expect something to be done in return.

There is no doubt that in the last ten years or so, the complications of school life have multiplied greatly, largely because, as you say, the young have so many more opportunities available, and it is marvellous that they should. But in the old days the sort of boy that came to our sort of school would go into his father's firm or profession; that is no longer true. They have to compete, and rightly so, for their jobs in the world, and there are so many more jobs available, not just the standard professions and occupations of their fathers, and so they are bewildered by the variety of employment ahead of them and by the variety of *standards* that they see about them, and coming over to them on the telebox, and so on.

McCulloch Do you think, in fact, that there is a curious lack of decision about what we fix as the 'age of responsibility' these days? In the Courts, for instance, people up to sixteen, I think it is now, are not held to be responsible—I mean, their parents have to take much more responsibility than used to be taken, and at the same time the Government, for some odd reason, has decided to lower the age at which the young have the responsibility to choose the Government. Isn't that odd?

McCrum It does strike one as a bit odd, although I think it is obviously two different groups of people approaching the problem from different angles. I would have thought that the first group, who are trying to ensure that the family are brought into the picture at an early stage, are absolutely right. At the other end I think there are many people who disagree with the Latey Commission Report quite strongly. The Latey Commission Report says that a young man can marry, and vote and is criminally responsible, and the rest of it, at eighteen, but my opinion is that the eighteen-year-old is certainly no more mature inwardly than he ever was before. Outwardly, because of National Health orange juice and plenty of milk when young and better food as he grows up, he is a bigger person than he was, inches taller than his father, and looks a great, confident, strapping young man; inwardly, however, he is just as insecure, just as much searching for guidance and a proper sort of authority as he ever was. And this is why I think it is a mistake to say that he can vote, that he can marry, and so on. I think the Latey Commission were too much influenced by the pressures of the groups representing the young.

McCulloch They do look more mature, you are right, but the more I know them, the more I am convinced that they are younger than we were at that particular age. They seem to me to be much less aware of any kind of framework in which to make decisions.

McCrum I think that is very true. Of course, the framework of tradition doesn't exist to the same extent today. So many more of them are the children of suburban homes where the family—and I mean by 'family', the *whole* family with grandparents, uncles and aunts—the old community, simply is no longer around. And therefore, not being brought up within a framework as large as that, the young are much more influenced, I believe, by the Press and other public media, particularly television. They know much more about important national and international issues than most of us, in this church, ever did when we were that age. These tremendous issues are thrust at them day by day, and they feel drawn into a larger world. This, in a sense, distracts them from the natural family framework, the morality of their family and their background. They are no longer so concerned, or so interested, in *that,* because they see much bigger issues coming in on them from outside.

McCulloch It didn't occur to me until you said that, that adolescence say, fifty years ago was fairly simple compared with what it is now. Admittedly there were the interior difficulties and so on, but it is true, I suppose, that they are more exposed today than we ever were.

McCRUM They *are* much more exposed, and I think very few boys—and presumably, girls also—would say today, at the end of their time at school, that these were the happiest days of their life. It wouldn't be true of any sensitive young person today to say that, because here is the age, *par excellence*, thirteen to eighteen, when you are suddenly becoming intensely aware of yourself and of other people, as persons, and being so intensely aware you feel the horrors and miseries of the world most acutely. As you know, the adolescent thinks more about death than almost anybody does until a good deal later on in life. Now he sees people being shot in front of his very eyes, assassinations taking place, starving children—all being constantly plugged at him, day after day, in the public media. It is not surprising, therefore, that he is bewildered, perplexed and upset.

McCULLOCH How does this react on the people who obviously must cope with his problems? You must get more questions than Thomas Arnold ever did!

McCRUM Well, I don't know about that. I've read Arnold's sermons and found them extraordinarily irrelevant to the present, but in his biography, you find him dealing with many of the same problems—the usual 'schoolboy' problems which, of course, constantly recur. But obviously he didn't have the awareness of the outside world to deal with, which we have today. I think this is what makes the job so fascinating, that you are not just stuck in a little inward-looking community, which our critics sometimes say Public Schools are, but you have got these people at the most creative stage of their lives and you can, perhaps, inject a little bit of order, of rationality, into a confused and irrational situation.

McCULLOCH What must complicate your task even further, I suppose, is that you have to produce the élite of the day, the kind of 'chosen' leaders. Presumably this is what Public Schools did, and still must do?

McCRUM I don't like the word 'élite'. Probably a lot of people here share my dislike.

McCULLOCH I used it deliberately.

McCRUM I know you did. It has become a dirty word, with some justification, I think, because it suggests an exclusivism, a sort of 'holier than thou' or rather a 'better than thou' atmosphere, which I think is horrible, and destructive of integrity and all the decent values of existence. So I object to the term 'élite', but I agree with you entirely in thinking that we have got to do something more than average. After all, people are paying a lot for the education we give; we cannot just teach 'A' level and 'O' level; we have got to do more than that. My feeling is, we want to produce something which one might call a creative minority. We want to turn out *people,* not types but individuals, who go into the world with a sense of responsibility, a sense of decision, an understanding and awareness of other people's needs. We want them to have a real social commitment and a conscience about the world, and my goodness, the world needs men with a conscience.

And so I would see the whole purpose of education, certainly in the boarding-schools, as creating a good deal more than just intellectual leaven in the lump; as trying to produce people who are going to be the salt—and salt is hurtful as well as healthy—to be the light, if you like, not on the hill because that suggests you are superior, but the light in the darkness down below. Those three well-known Biblical similes, I think, represent what I would like to see being turned out from any school I am associated with.

McCulloch I still pursue this word 'élite' although you have rejected it. I suppose that every society must look for a group of people who will give leadership in the various departments of its life. We used to have a very clear élite based on birth. That is to say, people were born into the circumstances which should destine them for leadership. Unfortunately, this élite was not necessarily notable for cerebral activity, and has since become discredited to a large extent. Leaving aside the word 'élite', if you prefer, do you still see it as the function of the Public Schools to produce this leadership group?

McCrum You see, I don't like this term 'leadership' much either, because, again, it suggests people *over* people. I don't mind people being led or leading; admittedly someone has got to set the pace, but this must be done by the most imaginative people, and I agree, if possible the best-trained minds. But I don't like the old idea of leadership from above and looking down on people; I want it to be on the shop-floor, alongside. Surely the difficulties of labour relations today emphasise that point. If leadership becomes too conscious a process of, as I say, being superior to other people, then I think it stinks.

McCULLOCH The occupant of the pulpit—the one you are in—last week, was Jack Jones. Do you think it would have been a good idea if he had been an old Etonian?

McCRUM I would think not because he probably wouldn't have become Jack Jones; he would have been the Honourable James Jones.

McCULLOCH Behind my rather frivolous question was an important one, and that is whether, in fact, the whole social change that is going on, and the shake-up of our social values, could affect, or be greatly affected by, the Public Schools during the next ten years, say?

McCRUM I don't myself think—and if there is a groan I shan't be surprised—I don't think that Public Schools really have anything to do with the class structure of this country. If you look around at other countries which have got no Public Schools—at France, for instance, which has a far more rigid class structure than our own, and as far as I know, only one well-known 'Public School'—you will see that class structure is something which is a creation of history, of the past of every country, and that it belongs to different countries in different ways. Our class structure is something which goes back in our history. Public Schools mirror it, they don't create it; I don't think they even reinforce it.

I see our role, among other things, as doing our best to liberate ourselves from anything which inhibits progress in our society, and I think that if you have a *rigid* class structure, this is likely to inhibit progress. I am not against class as such, because class so often simply means people who have the same interest getting together in order to share that interest. But if you start thinking of it in terms of jealousy and envy of what other people have got, it is very unhealthy. We can do quite a lot to try to point out to our young that they have no right to be superior because their parents happen to be richer. This sort of thing I think we *can* do and ought to do. But as we can't, for financial reasons, have a wider social cross-section—which most of us who teach in Public Schools would like to have—we are bound, I think, to go on to a certain extent as we are. But though class structure, as such, is not our business, it *is* something we want—not to undermine—but to show what the value of it is, and what the unpleasant side of it is. But I believe what really has done more to bring people in this country together are things like pop music, Marks and Spencer's clothes and such, where you automatically get a more homogeneous society, because our natural interests and our natural desires are met by modern mass-produced objects.

McCulloch Would you like to see the whole structure of the Public School system more broadly based? At the moment it is very difficult, isn't it, for a poor boy to be at a Public School?

McCrum Yes, it is difficult. At Tonbridge, where I am at the moment, we have a scheme by which a small number of boys from Primary Schools do come to us, and we provide them with scholarships and see them through their time at the school, and they are tremendously successful. It is a very good scheme and one just feels what an awful pity that one cannot extend it. The only limit to the extension of this scheme is shortage of money. As it is, it costs the School Governors a considerable amount of money each year, and they are only able to do this because of the wisdom of the Founder in leaving them some swamp land in London which now happens to be St Pancras! This is one of those blessings of the past which produces blessings in the present, and there is no doubt, from my experience of these boys who are in the school, that we should accommodate a great many more of them, to their good and our good. I am not, myself, in agreement with those who say that, in order to accommodate them, we would have to adapt our school society so tremendously that we would, in fact, destroy it. Nor am I in agreement with those who say that the boys coming into our sort of school would suffer a tremendous dislocation from the background from which they came. All I can say is that at Tonbridge, at any rate, this hasn't happened. We benefit and I believe they benefit. After all, we are a good school.

McCulloch The communication of values is presumably what you are after? How far does established religion help or hinder you?

McCrum That's a difficult one. There is much confusion and muddle in my generation about what we believe in, what we believe to be of real value and what we don't—as you can see on the television day after day—so if you can help to bring a little less confusion to people, then I think it is something that one ought to be doing. Indeed, it is something we try to do. Now, how far the established Church affects this process is a difficult one to answer. I think the Church obviously makes some difference; the trouble is, it is enmeshed in the trappings of the past, and has so much that is out-of-date about it. No one in his senses, looking at a bishop wearing gaiters and frock-coat, as I saw recently, at a dinner-party, can help but laugh. This is a ridiculous throwback, to make the bishops go on wearing this absurd garment. And much of the liturgy is terribly out of date. We adapt our school services, of course, but it is difficult to get the young to feel that religion is something alive and meaningful for their generation. We do try, we try very hard. There is more experimentation, I would say, going on in the Public Schools today than in the whole of the Church of England put together, even though the Church of England is experimenting quite a lot, as one can see here at this very moment.

McCULLOCH Would you agree that the one quality that one should encourage, not only in the young but in the middle-aged, is flexibility of mind? The great thing that keeps the Church back at the moment is just lack of flexibility of mind, I think, and if you could get the young to see that to *hold to Christ*—you know, that marvellous thing that Herbert Butterfield wrote, 'Hold to Christ, and for the rest, be totally uncommitted'—that that would be a terrific thing to do.

McCRUM I'm glad you quoted that. Flexibility of mind, *with* firmness of purpose and firmness of standards—those are the three things, it seems to me, you need. Yes, I would agree with you entirely.

McCULLOCH I must tell you that a friend of mine who was always girding at me about being a clergyman and who thought that the whole Church business was . . . well, we were on our way to the Reform Club where he was taking me to lunch, and as we were passing the Athenaeum he said, 'Don't look, Joseph, but over there is a man who has lost his horse', talking obviously of a bishop and his gaiters. I didn't look because I knew. I thought afterwards, I should have said, 'You are quite wrong, that is a man who is flogging a *dead* horse!'

By the way, very few bishops now wear gaiters. I ought to put that on record. And if the Public Schools are at all hampered by gaiters, they are under an illusion.

McCRUM Can I tell you a little story to counter yours? This was about two old Public School boys who had hated each other when they were at school, and they met on Bletchley station one day, later on in life. One of them, by this time, had become an Admiral, and the other one was a Bishop. Both were in their respective uniform. The Bishop went up to the Admiral, determined to make him feel small, as he always had at school, and he said, 'Stationmaster, can you tell me when the next train is?' And the Admiral, without even pausing, turned round to the Bishop—he was rather a portly Bishop—and said, 'Madam, in your condition I wouldn't recommend your catching the next train'.

McCulloch Which only goes to show that Public Schools are quite clearly abreast of the situation in the Church of England!

17 February 1970

The critics and reviewers almost invariably describe Tom Stoppard's work as brilliant. This remarkable consensus of expert opinion is evidently endorsed by discerning theatre-goers, who greet a new play of his by booking up every seat in the house long before the first night, and guarantee that it will have a long run. For it is still brilliant writing, before all else, which ensures good theatre.

People with scintillating minds are usually expected to be disconcerting company. They frequently are, simply because they tend to throw sparkling spanners into the works of dull conversation. If you are going to meet someone with a reputation of this kind, you prepare yourself rather like an average tennis-player about to encounter a Wimbledon star. On the whole we do not really like brilliant individuals; they have too much advantage of us, and we fear that they may take it.

Whatever substance there may be for such fear in some instances, they are quite groundless with Tom Stoppard. Nobody could be less showy in manner or less intoxicated with his own personality. He is the best of company, easy to talk with, constantly interested in what others have to say, totally unaffected and natural in conversation, but always, I would guess, acutely observant. It is for that reason, I would also guess, he is a born playwright, and now only in his thirties, has proved himself a master of the difficult craft of comedy.

Thornton Wilder said that a dramatist is one who from his earliest years has found that sheer gazing at the shocks and counter-shocks among people is quite sufficiently engrossing without having to encase it in comment. Tom Stoppard's comedies are sometimes described as moral plays. If so, it is not because he encases their action in moral comment. But he sees what is morally implicit in much that is going on around him, and his true brilliance is in enabling us also to see it as he does, with humanity and without dissimulation. No moralist, if Tom is one, was ever less dogmatic or more compassionate.

DIALOGUE WITH

Tom Stoppard

McCulloch I daresay many of you have already been to *Jumpers*. It was, without a doubt, more than anything for a very long time, what I mean by comedy, and I'm not saying that merely to say the right thing. I do mean it. It was very, very funny and yet had an underlying serious theme. When I say that many wives, including my own, have seen much of their husbands in your self-absorbed don, you will know how near the knuckle you got!

I am going to take a text from *Jumpers*, if you don't mind, from the last speech of the Professor of—was it Moral Theology, or something?

Stoppard Moral Philosophy.

McCulloch Moral *Philosophy*, which is worse—slightly. He says; 'A remarkable number of apparently intelligent people are baffled by the fact that a different group of apparently intelligent people profess to a knowledge of God, when commonsense tells *them*, the first group of apparently intelligent people, that knowledge is only a possibility in matters that can be demonstrated to be true or false, such as that the Bristol train leaves from Paddington.' Now, this seems to me the crunch of the modern world. Do you think this is true?

Stoppard I will tell you what was at the back of my mind in that speech. It is a fact that I know dozens of rational humanists who have a very hard-headed attitude to any mysticality in the theological tradition, and are very articulate and sceptical and scathing about it—*and read their horoscopes*. One does find that people accept horoscopes, not with any sort of firm conviction or absolute belief, but the very fact that horoscopes exist *at all* in a world which is said to be—at least in Western Europe—over sixty per cent non-church-going at best, suggests that everybody has a repository of a 'mystical' awareness that there is a lot more to them than meets the microscope. It's a difficult thing to express in terms which are not, if you like, 'spiritual' or 'mystical', but I think that almost everybody would admit to having this sense that some things actually are better than others in a way which is not, in fact, rational.

That, roughly, is the central concern of the play—*Jumpers*—if one can put it like that. But I am glad you called it funny, because I don't think it is very effective if it doesn't work as a comedy.

McCULLOCH Horace Walpole once said that the world is a comedy to those that think, and a tragedy to those that feel. Don't you think that it should have been, 'this world is a comedy to those that think they think'? What perhaps is worse, is that they think they think they *know*!

STOPPARD One knows what Walpole meant, and it is probably a little unfair to analyse too much because, of course, like a painter, he wishes to actually *convey* an idea. The outer edge may not be clearly defined, but as long as the message is central, that is enough.

McCULLOCH I am intrigued by your statement that it is unfair to analyse too much. Why?

STOPPARD A better word would have been 'irrelevant'. I think that as long as one understands what a man means by a statement, what he really *means*, then his failure to put it into a precise capsule which has absolutely no ambiguity about it, in a sense, doesn't matter. If you and I both know what we mean by *x*, then it doesn't actually matter if we express it ambiguously. That is all I meant.

McCULLOCH I would go further. I would say that, provided you and I think we like each other, or *feel* we like each other, then our words will not matter very much.

STOPPARD Oh, oh. I am not sure that I would think that I think that I know that I like you if we hadn't been able to communicate. It is not that you look so nice, is it?

McCULLOCH You would have to have oculist attention if you thought that! What I am trying to say is, that I have a profound suspicion, which seemed to me to ring out in *Jumpers*, and in other things you have written, that people who are clever, love to hear themselves being clever, but are not, in fact, saying anything very much.

STOPPARD You have a sort of anti-academic scepticism?

McCulloch I'm afraid so, yes. Ever since Oxford, I have been profoundly suspicious of academics.

Stoppard There is a lot to be said for an academic life. Goodness! the pulpit doesn't half make one pontifical.

I think that my definition of an academic person is not merely somebody who *lives* in a university, but whose major, professional preoccupation is a critical one towards other people's creative work, for example. There is a level of academic criticism which I think is its own justification, in that it gives an entirely innocent and entertaining occupation to a great number of people. I agree with you that much of it doesn't really have a useful application to that with which it presumes to be preoccupied. Some of it obviously does. Some academics are wholly admirable people—at any rate, they are people with admirable brains.

I think that the only thing which really puts me into an anti-academic frame of mind sometimes, is the sheer scale of the enterprise. I mean if there were a number of people here and there, innocently stimulated by analysing literature or doing some sort of demographic study of entirely hypothetical societies, I would find this absolutely fine—why not? But there are now millions of people studying a few hundred other people and their works, and the gearing is slightly ludicrous. They are living their whole lives in this sort of capsule, which I think feeds the brain and doesn't really feed the neighbours, if you see what I mean. The thought of those incredible American campuses, which are like cities full of people doing theses on Virginia Woolf, is quite monstrous. I don't know, when you use the word 'academic', whether you are using it in the sense that I am, as a writer. Perhaps you are thinking of other fields?

McCulloch No, I was thinking of the peculiar, introverted system in which I found myself at Oxford, where this curious idea that you could concentrate on a little piece of knowledge and assume that you *knew* something at the end of it, was extremely dangerous and misleading. I would go further and say that the great value of your play was that it revealed to most people who had not thought of it before, that man is never so comic as when he thinks about God.

Stoppard That's left me rather short of words. Is that a demonstrable proposition, or the opposite? It's an impression you have, is it—that it brings out the comic side of people?

McCULLOCH Yes. I mean, the moment that anybody starts to talk about whether God is, or is not, which your delightful professor did—Michael Hordern played him brilliantly, I thought—you show quite clearly how absurd we all are. If God *is*, then obviously our only possible justification could be that we exist in his mind. If God *is not*, then our bombinations about God, in a vacuum, don't matter at all.

STOPPARD Well, I don't suppose that there is anybody in the church now, who has never been confronted with that notion, at one time or another. But because—and this is the real problem, I think—one knows in advance that time, which will reveal all truths, is infinite, one actually begins with a hopeless quest, doesn't one?

McCULLOCH Is time infinite, by the way? Surely time *must* be finite?

STOPPARD On what grounds would you say that?

McCULLOCH Because time is obviously measurable, therefore it cannot be infinite.

STOPPARD It is one of those things with which I cannot bring myself to agree—such as that parallel lines meet at infinity.

McCULLOCH I hope *we* are not parallel lines! What I am trying to say is, that the moment a man begins to talk about God, instead of refraining his soul and just trying to love and worship God, he has become an absurdity.

STOPPARD Quite honestly, I would not have said that it brings out the comic side of people. I think it brings out, in a funny way, a sort of *embarrassed* side about them, because it is not really an area which gets much exposure. I think that there is a central confusion. You and I, even now, are talking about God in a way which has nothing to do with religion as such, nothing even to do with worship. I think that the kind of questions which ordinary people ask themselves, are the questions which actually give rise to academic philosophy: academic philosophy doesn't give rise to these questions. So when you make the sort of statement that you have just made about people thinking about God, surely they are doing so in ways which are bringing up questions of logical possibility, rather than a sort of mystical instinctive conviction about a Supreme Being.

McCULLOCH It is precisely what you meant in the last part of *Jumpers*. Surely it is the limiting of knowledge to one particular method of objective observation which makes man ridiculous at present. The scientist is the most ridiculous of men the moment he strays outside the question of 'How does this thing work?' But what it is for and indeed the whole problem of ends, is right outside the scientist's purview. This has led the twentieth century astray more than anything else. Pulpits *are* places where you pontificate—you have said precisely that.

STOPPARD I rather think that science and theology will always find a way to dance together to the music, because the whole of science can be said, by a theologian, to be operating within a larger framework. In other words, the higher we penetrate into space and the deeper we penetrate into the atom, all it shows to a theologian is that God has been gravely underestimated. In Galileo's time the view that the earth was at the centre of the universe, and everything else went around it once a day, meant that the whole thing could not be that big, however fast it was all going; it had to be a reasonable size; and in the still centre of this mechanism was the apple of God's eye. The awful thing about a *rotating* earth was that suddenly the whole machine became infinitely huge. There was no reason for it to stop anywhere at all, and, to quote Brecht, 'In such a universe, even the Pope might lose the eye of God'. It is the thought that suddenly one was no longer this privileged little unique world in the middle of these marble globes, but that one was simply on a lump of rock, barely distinguishable from millions of others, flung out into unimaginable space like a dice flung out of a cup—it was this, surely which upset the theologians of the time. And I think the lesson which derived from that confrontation was the thought that God *had* been underestimated and that all this changed nothing. It simply, as it were, glorified God.

MCCULLOCH I think that God *is now* beginning to be underestimated, not *has been*. In the Middle Ages they had an *Organum*, the idea of the whole in which all branches of knowledge had their proper place. Today we have got analysts of various kinds, all breaking down knowledge into tiny little bits, and having no context into which to fit each. The idea that space, size, and so on should be important is a *modern* idea. I mean, no decent medieval theologian was worried about the *size* of things. This is much more a modern idea.

STOPPARD Is it?

MCCULLOCH Oh, surely. What does it matter how big space is, or how small the micro-organism is? Does it matter? It only goes to show how totally compendious the mind of God is.

STOPPARD I think it is one of those things which doesn't matter now because the thing is demonstrably huge. I'm not sure that in the early seventeenth century it was of such little concern.

MCCULLOCH Perhaps I can make clearer my main point by asking another question. Your play portrays a philosopher who does marvellous mental acrobatics. But isn't the far more marvellous thing the fact that he should exist at all? Isn't that the real question he raises in himself?

STOPPARD I can accept everything about him in purely mechanistic terms except one thing. I can accept the evolution of the tripes and pipes and liquids which are in him. I can accept the evolution of the button on his cuff and the cathode-ray tube he watches, and everything about him—except his ability to discuss it, because there, to me, is a break in—what would you call it—philosophical logic, perhaps? There is a gap between an object becoming as complex, as prolific, as intelligent and as extraordinary as it can be, of itself, and actually *knowing* all these things about itself. This seems to me, in the imagery in which it occurs to me, to create a gap where you need to make a jump.

MCCULLOCH Is there not something peculiarly missing in your Professor Moore that makes him comic? Is there not something that makes me or anybody else, comic? Wherever I trip up and am not humble, when I am not confronting the universe and saying, 'God, how magnificent', I reduce myself to absurdity. 'Whoso exalteth himself shall be abased.' Jesus was always pointing to the comic aspect of our tragic situation, where we become so above ourselves that we no longer can become what we really are.

STOPPARD Yes, but this is talking of comedy on a much more elevated plane than I practise it. I actually do two things: I write comedy but I also write jokes.

MCCULLOCH So did Jesus—at least, he spoke them. But he wasn't box-office then!

STOPPARD I don't think that I really go along with you on the importance you give to the comic aspect of things. Because to me it is not the important thing. It is the cart in front of the horse, in a way.

MCCULLOCH What's the horse? The tragedy?

STOPPARD No, that is really the point. I don't actually see it in those terms. I ought to say briefly, so you can just know it and forget it, that one has to bear in mind, in writing for the theatre, that one is also actually involved with a lot of practical problems which are nothing to do with philosophy, comedy, art, drama or anything else. They are entirely to do with actually writing the next line and doing something which will keep people in a room reasonably preoccupied and interested—the practical things.

I must say that until *Jumpers*, I had never set out to write a play about an idea. In every other case, I've written plays about specific people in a specific situation, and ideas tended to be the end-product of the play, rather than *vice versa*. Something between the two happened in *Jumpers*. What I am saying is, that the notion of seeing cosmic comedy in those terms, as something which one can, as it were, have in the back of one's mind while one is writing, doesn't really happen. I know what you mean and I can see why you see it in the text, but in a way, it is not part of the play for me; it is not part of the *writing*.

McCULLOCH One final question, perhaps an unfair one. Viewing the modern mind, and seeing that it is totally analytical—always trying to take the motor car to pieces while it is on the way—would you, if you were really sick, which you are not, but if one *was* sick, that is to say, bewildered in one's mind, would you rather have two years with a psychoanalyst, or five minutes with a priest—a good priest, by the way?

STOPPARD I would much rather have five minutes with a priest, but not necessarily for the reasons you would wish me to give. You may not accept that my reason might be simply that I don't have two years for anybody. To answer this question fairly, I share some of your scepticism about mind-medicine.

McCULLOCH But if you had the chance of going to someone you believed—although he was just a person like yourself—was speaking in the name of one who said, 'Go and sin no more; neither do I condemn thee', wouldn't that be a more wholesome thing than having yourself taken to pieces and your mind concentrated upon your own ego, as must happen a great deal in psychiatry?

STOPPARD I think it *is* an unfair question, because you must be more empirical than that. I don't want to be evasive but I don't really *want* to answer that question, because it is too serious a question to answer in a very brief, flippant way.

I think two things: first of all, about professions which deal with human welfare and particularly mental welfare—it is unknown territory in which a lot of people appear, perhaps, to be obsessives, who are actually feeding something into themselves. On the other hand, all progress which is broadly beneficial, of course has within it odd people whom one doesn't trust—which doesn't really matter. I think, generally speaking, that psychiatry is of inestimable worth to society, and that one person in ten probably needs it.

What you are really asking me, is what are the important things. Here is somebody else's answer. After a philosophic lecture, in which, I think, a lot of things which we have said were incorporated, somebody said to the speaker, 'I think that everything you say is true, but is it important?' and this philosopher replied, 'I'm not at all sure that importance is important—but Truth is'.

20 March 1973

Politics is a profession particularly prone to the changes and chances of this fleeting world, so much so that one would expect politicians to become inevitably disillusioned and cynical. But there is no sign of James Callaghan's being so. He probably has lost most of his illusions, after many years in and out of office. But he sails on cheerfully, on a very even keel for the most part, and, even when things get rough, maintains his imperturbable good temper towards friend and foe alike. He appears the exemplar of the stoic ideal of ataraxia, the refusal to be put out of countenance—a man disinclined to extremes, who prefers to steer patiently along the line of commonsense towards the objective of greater social democracy.

But this is by no means to say that he is easy-going or complaisant. His life has never allowed him the effortless inertia of those born to wealth, inherited status or patronage. Hence, in maintaining a position or principle he can be very difficult to dislodge and resolutely tough in resistance. But even in his aggressiveness, when he moves over to the attack, the pleasant irony which the discerning may always detect in the expression of his eyes is still there. Even at the height of over-heated controversy, he can cool the temperature by good-humouredly calling his opponent's bluff in such a way that the argument returns to the level of rational discussion. For that reason, *inter alia*, he is one of the best-liked personalities in the Commons.

His value in terms of ability and experience both in the Labour party and in the nation's affairs ensures that he will continue to play a considerable role on the stage of politics, not least because his vision is not narrowly confined to the merely partisan or even national interest. His eyes are on the world; his concern is with the problems all mankind must solve only by recognizing their common involvement in them. He has the gift of being able to think on his feet, but even what he says off the cuff, as we found, is likely to give us much to ponder, whatever our political bias.

DIALOGUE WITH

James Callaghan

McCULLOCH There has been so much anticipation of Mr Callaghan's visit that people have been telling me what *not* to talk about, and I was reminded, in the last week, of the time when I was first married. My wife had two brothers; one had become a very argumentative, active, left-wing chap and the other was equally argumentative about religion, and we had a notice—you know, one of those 'IN—OUT' things, and when they came to stay —they were both up at Oxford at the time—we used to have 'No Politics by Request' on one side and 'No Religion by Request' on the other. So that left us quite free to talk happily about anything under the sun barring those two subjects.

Well, various people have been telling me what *not* to talk about, and then one man stopped me in Cheapside the other day and said, 'When Mr Callaghan comes, please ask him what is happening to *us*'—that is to say, I presume, the British people. Well, I think that is a fair question. Are we as bad as they say we are? Are we fundamentally changed as a people?

CALLAGHAN Am I supposed to answer that? Well, let me say to begin with, just to try to invite a little sympathy, that I don't think I have ever felt so nervous as I do now, standing up here! I suppose politicians do preach, but certainly not in elevated pulpits like this, and I would have thought, with respect, that you might have bowled me an easier one for the first question!

Are we the same people we always were? The answer is clearly, 'No'! We can't be, because all of us are shaped, not wholly but to some extent, by the pace of change, which is faster today than it has ever been in the lifetime of any generation. People are having to adapt to that very rapidly indeed. But on the other hand, yes, we are the same people we always were. Let me give you an example.

A very nice thing happened to me, literally this morning, and I didn't know that the Rector was going to ask me this question, but when I went into the House of Commons and looked at my mail, there was an envelope lying there, which said: 'J. Callaghan M.P., Kingly Street, W.1. 1 mile charged for 2 miles, 20p. returned.'

Now, I found myself wondering what it was all about and then I remembered. About ten days ago, I went to the Independent Television News studios up in Kingly Street and I asked the taxi-driver when I got out how much it was, and I paid him, and quite clearly he must have charged me twenty pence too much. And this morning there was the envelope with the twenty pence in it waiting on my desk. Well now, I think that is, amid all the prevailing gloom, something worth putting on the other side, because it shows that although we are having to adapt ourselves, as a people, to very changed technological circumstances, the traditional values that we grew up with have not entirely disappeared.

McCULLOCH That's very nice! Now in the eighteenth century, Montesquieu came here, and was staying in this country as a guest, and he wrote back to France: 'These are a great people. They understand three things—commerce, liberty and religion.' Do you think you would say that, if you wrote about us these days?

CALLAGHAN I don't think, in your presence, I ought to comment on religion too much, but I think this does hinge to some extent on your previous question, as to whether we are changing.

I think in commerce, clearly, we are extremely able. After all, who would *dare* come here to the City, and say we weren't! Yes, I think our reputation is a good one, although perhaps we over-value it sometimes and think that people here are so much better than everywhere else in the world, which isn't wholly true. But nevertheless, of course we do understand commerce very well indeed, as we did in the eighteenth century.

As to freedom—yes. I was very glad indeed to see the spontaneous reaction to the conviction and imprisonment of Peter Nieswand. People feel deeply indignant that a man should have been arrested, put on trial without the charges ever being made public, not even known to his wife, and that he should be convicted without a jury being present. I think this caused a wave of revulsion which is indicative of the British approach to the problem of speech and liberty.

But, coming back to this problem of change you were talking about. I think in some ways we are changing back to what we were when Montesquieu made his comments in the eighteenth century. The nineteenth century was, in its way, a temporary historical aberration, in the sense that we developed the Empire—the greatest Empire the world has ever seen—and it did a lot of good, though it had a lot of blots on it too, obviously. When you think of the life of the British Empire it really is, as against a number of other empires, a pretty short period of time. After all, our Empire in Africa lasted only fifty or sixty years. But I think those of us who are old enough to remember the days of Empire, tend to think that we *always* had a great Empire, and were the leaders of the world, in this sense, and therefore there *is* a feeling of defeatism among some of the older generation, that we aren't any longer living up to that. Now, of course, if we get into that attitude of mind we are going to be a pretty paranoic lot, and the British people aren't like that. I would prefer to believe that Montesquieu spoke the truth about us. It is traditionally the kind of people we *were* that lasted through Tudor and Elizabethan days, right up through Cromwell and the rest of it, to the time when we had this nineteenth century flowering, if you like, of Empire. Now, I think, from various signs we are reverting to the kind of people that we were.

McCULLOCH But there seems to be certain problems in our character that are not yet resolved. I am inclined to think that they are due to overcrowding. I think that there are too many people on the island at the moment. I don't know what the answer to that is, but it's clear that because of overcrowding, certain aspects of our character: tolerance, politeness, civic sense and so on, seem to be in danger. Am I wrong?

CALLAGHAN Not wholly. I would have thought there was a great deal of truth in that. When my mother was born, this country had a population of about thirty-five million people and was capable of feeding itself. Now of course, our history was distorted by the growth of population in the early part of the twentieth century and I think, myself, that if this country had thirty-five to forty million people living in it, instead of the fifty-three million we've got, we would find much more elbow-room for all of us.

Now you can say, 'What is to be done about it?' Obviously family planning is a way in which you can begin to tackle this problem, and I certainly don't think it is our job to procreate as many children as we can, as a matter of *duty* any more! But of course, the experts can be wrong in their predictions. One never knows about these things. I have seen many projections about the future of the population, several of which contradict each other, and I would say we had better take them all with a grain of salt. But if we *could*, by a system of family planning, make sure that our population runs at just about the same level, well and good. Indeed, in an ideal Britain, I think I would prefer to see it smaller than it is.

McCULLOCH Yes. What about the question of apathy—what the

theologians call *accidie*—the kind of tiredness that comes in the noonday? Is it true that the mood of our people today is that kind of apathy? We're obviously religiously apathetic. Are we also becoming politically apathetic.

CALLAGHAN Ah, difficult one! I don't know. I could find evidence on both sides for that. I think what has happened is that the opinion-makers in the country—the 'Establishment', if you like—have lost faith. I come back to this question of the Empire. There used to be a very clear coherent view that the leaders of opinion in this country had. The British Empire was a very simple conception and—you know, all that red on the map—in a way, it dyed our minds. When we lost the Empire, we tried to replace it by a conception of Commonwealth, and that was going to be the great thing. But then we found that the African countries wanted to escape from the leading-strings, and go their own way; Australia and New Zealand did; Canada in particular wanted to escape, so the idea of the Commonwealth faded away. Then we turned to Europe. Now, I know that there are many people whom I like and respect, who really have a vision about Europe; I'm sorry to say I don't share it. It is a useful and convenient way of organizing our relations with Europe, and in matters of commerce and trade it is obviously a worthwhile instrument. But it is not a vision in the way that the Empire was a vision, the way people hoped that the Commonwealth would be, and I think that a lot of our opinion-makers in the Press and elsewhere are now a bit fogged. They have found that Europe doesn't really live up to their expectations. Commonwealth gone, Empire gone—what do they do? And therefore I think that there is, in fact—I use your word, 'apathy'—a sense of where-do-we-go-from-here?

But I don't find that in my constituency in Cardiff. There's no sense of apathy there. People are living a fuller, and a more enjoyable and richer life than they did when I first became their Member nearly thirty years ago. There are many more opportunities open to them; of going out at the weekend in the car, of listening to classical music, of all sorts of activities which never existed thirty years ago.

MCCULLOCH I was wondering whether that, in itself, isn't a cause of political apathy? You see, people are having—as you quite rightly said—much fuller lives than they had and they are rather apt to leave the politics, the actual government of the country and so on, to other people. They don't want to be bothered.

CALLAGHAN I think to some extent we are responsible for this.

One of the reasons for political apathy is the feeling that it is difficult to influence decisions, and therefore people are turning in on themselves more than they used to. This is why it is possible, as it would not have been thirty years ago, to fight and win an election almost on the issue of paving-stones, as was done recently. Because people feel that paving-stones are something that they do know about and can do something about.

Now, one of the great problems which is going to arise—and I am glad to have this opportunity of making this point—is that I think Parliament, which was fought for, our democratic rights which were won after a Civil War, after a battle with the Sovereign and a later battle with the Lords—I think these powers of Parliament are now dwindling and are likely to dwindle very fast. I am very proud of our Parliament at Westminster, proud to be a politician, which I think is one of the greatest tasks anyone can have. But I tell you, this is something I fear for the next generation. All of us ought to be conscious of what is happening. There is a two-way stretch in Parliament now—one way the stretch is going, is to Brussels, and Members are now absenting themselves from Parliament in order to go to the European Parliament, and so the life of our Parliament is—I won't put it too hard—but it *is* somewhat diminished. Now, that is one stretch. The other stretch is into the regions. One of the things I've seen since I've been in the House, is the great growth of regional pride. When I first went into the House, there were the specialized committees or groups—the energy group, the transport group, the foreign group—which attracted all the attention. Now it is the regional groups that are well-attended; they are the lively, effective, hard-working bodies—the Welsh group, the Scottish group and the rest of it. This is the second part of the two-way stretch; people are feeling they can influence matters in their own region and therefore are turning more and more in that direction. Meanwhile the life-blood of Parliament, to some extent, is draining away.

Now, I may be absolutely wrong about this, because I am forecasting, but I think it could be that in ten to fifteen years' time, Parliament may be very different from the one that we grew up with and worked for. I don't want to be old-fashioned, but I still think we *want* a United Kingdom, I still think the best thing is to focus it on Westminster. And I fear that unless we all consciously take this problem in hand and say, 'What are we going to do about it?' we may find that, by default, people look to Brussels, to Cardiff, to Edinburgh, to Newcastle, and that Westminster may be squeezed out.

McCULLOCH Very interesting indeed. Tell me, what do you think are the three most important internal problems of this country which have to be solved in the next ten or fifteen years?

CALLAGHAN I think, first of all, I would put the question of race relations. It is simmering underneath very much and I think we have all got to try to understand it. When I was Home Secretary, I had no doubt that it was my job to regulate the flow of people coming in, and I was very heavily attacked in some quarters for doing that. I believed then that that was right and, with respect to those who are arguing a different case, I think so now. We've got a large number of coloured people living here; they can live here peacefully, and—I'm sorry to keep reverting to Cardiff—but we've had coloured people living in Cardiff, as some of you may know, since the First World War, and they are in the community, part of the community and living happily. We are going to be a different society, that is clear, with this great admixture of people, but if we don't scratch at the problem too much, if we work at it, then I think it can be solved amongst ourselves. I would put that as problem number one—not in a hopeless sense, as some people do, but simply as a problem that has got to be solved.

The second problem, I think, is that of unemployment and the disparity between the regions. I speak as a regional M.P. and I think that the way in which 4,000 men can now learn, as they did in my constituency on 29 December, that the steel-works is to be closed, is simply something which a modern society can't tolerate. There have got to be new methods here and they have got to be pretty draconian. The free market simply cannot now assume all the social obligations of providing work; there must be much more *purposeful* government intervention in the activities of great companies and institutions. In simple human terms, people will not tolerate now being put out on the streets and told there is no future or no jobs. They say, 'Look here, if society cannot organize itself better than that, we want a different society'. That is the second problem that I would enumerate.

The third immediate problem is housing. I once talked to an old Catholic priest who was the mayor of his little town in Italy and he said—he was a socialist—'I'll tell you what my definition of socialism is—it is a home to live in, a job to go to, a school to be educated in, a hospital when you are sick and a church to worship in.' Now this was his definition—very, very simple, and I am trying to talk in these terms.

Housing, I think, is a monstrous problem, and if we are going to get the situation right, there ought to be a conscious national effort *now* to, I would say, double the number. I read in the paper this morning, 110 or 120 thousand houses are to be started this year. There ought to be, in my view, at least 200,000 if we could get there.

I think if you could deal with these simple problems for people, and if every family in this land could get a home to live in at a reasonable price, then you have at least provided the basis for a happy society. Society demands a lot more non-material things than that, as you well know, but I won't go into them for the moment.

McCULLOCH The other thing that faces this country is our role in the world. What part do you see Great Britain playing in the next, say, fifteen to twenty years?

CALLAGHAN I want us to raise our eyes from Europe. Maybe the European incident was important and necessary, but we have got a larger and wider tradition than merely the regard of Europe. Even before our Empire days this was true. After all, Walter Raleigh set out from here, and others have too, and I think that we have got a role to play in the rest of the world.

I would like to see the Commonwealth strengthened. I have discussed this with some Commonwealth statesmen. I think it was natural that, as they became independent they wanted to break away, but you see, the Commonwealth has got great virtues. It means that there is one meeting-place for nations that are black and white, and rich and poor. Now, these two problems of black and white, and rich and poor, among the nations of the world, are going to assume enormous importance in the next twenty to thirty years. So I would like therefore, to see the Commonwealth strengthened, if we can get a response, and if we have sufficient imagination.

Beyond that, it is, perhaps, somewhat astonishing, when one travels abroad, to see how much people in other countries are willing to listen to us. They know we haven't got the power of the U.S.S.R. or China or the United States, but they still feel that we have got *experience*. Perhaps we have had rather longer looking at and understanding their problems than some other people have, and certainly we haven't got the particular vested interests that some other people now have. And I think that if Britain now, while obviously regularising her affairs with Europe, were to look a bit wider again, to the rest of the world, I think we should find a response there. This isn't to say that we are going to be a great power or anything like that, but we would find that people would be very interested about our attitude and our reactions to their particular problems. I found this particularly in South East Asia.

McCULLOCH My final question. Do you see us then, as playing what I would think is the most important of all roles, that of a reconciling power?

CALLAGHAN I think less a reconciling power and more a power that understands both sides. Maybe that might lead to reconciliation, perhaps you are right, but certainly I feel that to understand the problem is the beginning of being able to reconcile, and I would say, without putting ourselves into a false position, that we could play a role in that way.

10 April 1973

It is an irony of our modern communications that Diana Rigg became known and admired in many countries through a television series. No actress was ever more dedicated to the living stage, as she has since proved beyond cavil to the delight of countless theatre-goers. My wife and I first met her when she received us back-stage before an evening performance of *Abélard and Héloise*. A few days later she was coming to us to take part in the dialogue which follows.

The litmus paper which dichotomizes the famous in any walk of life is whether they seek primarily success or achievement. This is by no means a distinction without a difference, although it may appear so to the unreflective. When I describe Diana as dedicated, I mean that from my knowledge of her, to give a good performance of a demanding part satisfies her ambition more than to win applause by a facile piece of acting. And it is not only on the stage she asks of life deep waters. In the mediocrity of subtopia she would soon die of boredom. And nobody I know is less tolerant of the deadly virtues.

On stage she can be terrifyingly brilliant, as I saw her in the last performance of *Jumpers* at the Old Vic, out-Marilyning Monroe. But at supper afterwards she was warm, unaffected, fundamentally serious, highly intelligent, emotionally plumb honest, a truly female woman. Diana is totally uninterested in the ploys of femininity. I imagine that she is devastating to the male who treats her as anything other than a person in her own right.

Yes, I admire her unreservedly. But not merely because she is endowed with attributes which satisfy the aesthetic sense. What I most enjoy in her is a genuine struggle for personal integrity and spiritual freedom. That seems to me before everything else what makes another person worth knowing, although at times it may involve a clash of contraries. 'Without Contraries,' said William Blake, 'is no progression.'

DIALOGUE WITH

Diana Rigg

McCULLOCH When my wife and I saw Diana Rigg in *Abélard and Héloise*—which I suppose is one of the most wonderful stories in history—I thought it was a great triumph for Miss Rigg, because of all historical parts, I would think that Héloise was one of the most difficult. It stimulated my mind so much that I have been thinking about it ever since.

Now, tell me, what do you think the real issue is, in this story of Abélard and Héloise?

RIGG I think, basically, it is about the predicament of Abélard. He belonged to the *Civitas Dei*, which was an Order whose members, although they didn't take vows of continence, in the eyes of the world were expected to be continent.

McCULLOCH Let us get the word 'continent' clear. You mean Abelard shouldn't have had anything to do with a woman?

RIGG No, nothing at all. And he fell in love with Héloise. They had a very deep and very passionate relationship. It seemed that after thirty-seven years of celibacy, he was trying, in fact, to pack everything into the short time they had together. Héloise, on the other hand, understood far more than he did the issues that their relationship would throw up. In other words, she was very modern, she understood that they could not flaunt their love, they could not get married, she was even content to remain, in the eyes of the world, his harlot, and a terrible predicament was set up there: his attitude of wishing to make their love honest and open and hers, in realizing that in so doing he would ruin himself.

McCULLOCH This was quite clearly a twelfth century problem, wasn't it? Or do you think this is something that could arise in the twentieth century?

RIGG Oh yes, I think it is still with us. Why, only today, in the papers, the Roman Catholic Primate of Belgium made a statement on celibacy in the Church.

McCULLOCH But it isn't only in the Roman Catholic Church, is it? I mean, it is quite a common problem. Very often a couple can't marry for some reason—say, for instance, that it will ruin a man's career—and the woman sees it as her job to sacrifice herself. Isn't that what Héloise did, really?

RIGG I wouldn't call it sacrifice. I think women, in loving totally, are prepared to give everything, and to call it a sacrifice would put it on a pedestal. Sacrifice would suggest giving up something that you care for very deeply. Héloise cared only for Abélard.

McCULLOCH Yes, but she had to give up a great deal else. Don't you think perhaps you have a romantic view of sex? When all is said and done, what is sex? It is a means of producing the next generation.

RIGG I don't understand that. I think sex is not simply procreation, I don't think it ever has been, nor ever will be.

McCULLOCH If it is not merely for procreation, what is it for?

RIGG Well, it is another form of communication, for one thing.

McCULLOCH Oh, but I can communicate without sex.

RIGG Anybody *can* communicate without sex. I'm not saying sex is the *most* important thing, but it is very, very important.

McCULLOCH You see, what I am driving at is simply this—I'm agreeing with you really—that what one is looking for in life is a kind of wholeness of personality, fullness of life. Do you agree with that?

RIGG Yes.

McCULLOCH Presumably sex, therefore, is one way of achieving this wholeness and obviously, between men and women it must be. In the animal world sex *is* merely for procreation, but something new has arrived in the nature of sex in the human race—the whole of man's mind. We are a race that, for good or ill, has to make some sort of marriage between emotion and reason. That is what is so important about Abélard, isn't it? He was trying hard to do just that. He didn't succeed, I don't think, do you?

RIGG No, because he had the machinery of the Church against him.

McCULLOCH Well, the Church at that time was going through a very important period of its life. It was trying to sweat out of its system the paganism, the whole permissiveness of the Roman civilization which had collapsed. Every age that goes off the deep end about this particular thing, always has to spend a hundred years or so sweating it out of its system, and getting back to a kind of balance. The Middle Ages were precisely such a period and Abélard came up in that situation, didn't he?

RIGG When you say 'get back to a kind of balance', what do you mean, precisely?

MCCULLOCH I think we have to work out for ourselves what freedom really means. You see, the Victorians got us into a strait-jacket and not only the Victorians—we are suffering from the whole inheritance of puritanism. Now, sensuality is a good word. By sensuality, I mean the satisfaction of the senses. I am a very sensual person. I love good things, and I think that is right. But obviously if you are going to satisfy the senses, you have got to develop a kind of taste and a discipline.

RIGG In order to satisfy the senses, I would imagine, you have to have a spectrum of experience, and experiment and discriminate for yourself, surely? This is what they now call permissiveness.

MCCULLOCH No, what they now call permissiveness—well, they're all over the place, aren't they? A very delightful girl said to me the other day, 'The real problem for our generation is that we have got too many choices and we are bewildered'.

RIGG I think that is a tragedy—that she should feel bewildered, I mean. In my adolescence I had very little choice.

MCCULLOCH I think you were probably lucky! The real point, surely, is that we ought to be able to train human personality so that it knows where the satisfaction of the senses lies.

RIGG No, you can't possibly do that because people are individual. You can't train a mass of individuals. Discovering one's sensuality is something which is a very, very personal process. You can't make rules that apply to everybody.

MCCULLOCH Why not? Alec Douglas-Home said something very important in that pulpit once. He said, it seemed to him that what mattered was that one should ask oneself whether one's course of action will harm anybody else. Isn't that a rule that applies to everybody?

RIGG That is a humanist rule; it's not necessarily a sensualist rule.

McCULLOCH Oh yes it is. It applies everywhere, I think. The question is, whether what I do does harm or good. Abélard, when he crashed into Fulbert's house, surely did a terrible thing. You see, I think that what Abélard hated himself for was what he did to Fulbert—you know, he went to this old man who loved his niece, and he got himself taken into that house, and he abused his hospitality, didn't he? He seduced the niece. Roughly speaking, that is what we would say today. Well, that was his problem. He hated himself for doing that. And Héloise understood that.

RIGG That was the pedestrian problem—a problem of embarrassment, of good faith that he had destroyed. But he had a far greater problem, in fact, which was that of the man who discovered the sensual life and couldn't reconcile it with his intellectual life. One or the other had to be sacrificed and he sacrificed his intellectual life.

McCULLOCH I'm not sure that you're not over-simplifying; I think it was deeper than that. I think he knew a lot about the sensual life. A man can't get to thirty-seven with the brain that he had without knowing a great deal.

RIGG Well, it must have been a vicarious knowledge, mustn't it?

McCULLOCH Anyhow, he fell in love with this beautiful girl, and I think, knew that he either had to say yea to it or nay. He said yea, but he did it in such a way that he betrayed himself in doing so. And I think that good sensuality is when you can keep your integrity *and* enjoy your senses. And this is what the young today are looking for, aren't they? The formula whereby you keep your integrity and enjoy the senses.

RIGG I don't think 'integrity' is a word which would mean very much to them, do you?

McCULLOCH Oh, I think they're looking for integrity like mad. I don't think they've found it but I think they are a deeply sincere generation. And they are looking desperately. But there is another word that comes up in the Abélard and Héloise story, and that is the word 'chastity'. In these days, as you know, chastity is a bad word, something you run away from. But surely all it means is that you keep yourself with integrity in a situation; you don't betray yourself. Abélard did, and he hated himself afterwards.

RIGG Chastity means that? I thought it meant . . .

McCULLOCH Oh yes, I know, you thought it meant just not going to bed with somebody outside wedlock.

RIGG No, no, no. I thought that chastity meant a very strict discipline where maybe your desires might lead you in one direction, and you disciplined yourself so that you didn't take—for instance—that second helping of whatever it is, or your second glass of wine. That is chastity.

MCCULLOCH Yes, but chastity means even more than that. It means emotional honesty, and I think if you can keep emotional honesty—it's very difficult to do—but it is surely the best thing that you *can* do, isn't it?

RIGG Indeed, but the wheel has come full circle now, because our discussion fifteen minutes ago was about sex and sexual attitudes as they are now, and I would say that emotional honesty is perhaps one of the strongest factors in the sexual attitudes of today.

MCCULLOCH I am absolutely with you. I think that you cannot divorce sexual life from personal integrity. This is where your play raises the great questions again and it is important for that reason. Why do we do certain things, how do we really express honesty in them? Why couldn't Abélard and Héloise have gone off and got married, that is the first question.

RIGG Simply because he was a man who was, before he met her, committed to a course in life which did not admit cohabitation with a woman, did not admit loving a woman or giving her a child.

MCCULLOCH Should there ever be any situation in human life where you cannot marry a woman you love?

RIGG I would have thought not ever.

MCCULLOCH So would I. That is why I am against a rule of celibacy. I think it is wrong and I hope the Archbishop of Belgium will get his point. It is important for the Roman Church. But, at the same time, don't let us ride away on that. The attempt to be a priest *and* be married is a jolly difficult one.

RIGG Yes, but I would have thought that with the knowledge of a relationship with a woman, and the weakness and problems, his attitude towards the people who came to see him would be far more realistic, far more humane.

MCCULLOCH I agree. And I think it important for a man to have a woman to interrupt his airy-fairy; keep him *earthed*, so to speak, as you are doing! But at the same time, if you are trying to get integrity of a very high order—which they were in the twelfth century—a woman is a distraction, an interruption in the attempt to get an intense purity of motive. I think we have seen through that, now. It was a negative, wasn't it? But we haven't yet found a positive way, not quite. I mean, in the Church, we have married clergy, and on the whole they perform good service in the community, but it is still true to say that the fact that the priest has a wife, makes people very often not come to him, you know, because—well, because wives are often so close to their husbands, and I suppose there is a fear that the husbands might betray the seal of the confessional, or something.

RIGG I wouldn't have thought so.

MCCULLOCH No, but this is what people feel. Do you see what I mean? It is still not solved.

RIGG But might not a married priest—providing, of course, that the relationship was a good one—have a two-fold force? Because he would have the feminine force as well as his own male force and, I would have thought, for a person in need of help or counsel, that would be the perfect man to go to.

MCCULLOCH Would you say that women should be priests?

RIGG I think this is questionable. I hate to be sort of feminist about this or anti-feminist but I would never go to a woman priest for advice or counsel. I think very few women would.

MCCULLOCH Would you rather have been educated by a man rather than a woman?

RIGG Yes.

MCCULLOCH I think you are right. I think that where we are lacking at the moment in our education, is that we don't give enough attention to the cross-reference, as it were—that men and women should educate both boys and girls. You agree about that?

RIGG Yes, very much. I think for a child—for a young girl—the observation of man and male, and the opportunity to talk and communicate on an asexual level is terribly important. And this would apply to boys also, being taught by women.

MCCULLOCH May I ask you this? At the moment, the great worry of a great many people is that sex gives out, as it were. I mean, there are various reasons, why a sexual relationship becomes out of joint or doesn't work any more, and people think that is the end of the line. Do you believe that?

RIGG No, I don't think it is true, but there again, it is up to the individual. I couldn't begin to talk or philosophise. I know what I feel and it is quite personal and quite profound. I think you have to discover a way for yourself. Nowadays two people confront each other initially, and then perhaps go away and make love quite soon, after the first, second or third encounter. And it is only *after* that sexual obstacle has been overcome—in other words, once they have realised each other physically, sensually—that the relationship starts and develops. This is a complete inversion of what it was some fifty or sixty years ago.

McCULLOCH But supposing it doesn't develop?

RIGG Then it is called a mistake, just as a marriage can be a mistake.

McCULLOCH But does this affect the integrity of the person?

RIGG Not at all. It seems to me that they have got their priorities right.

McCULLOCH I'm not trying to be dogmatic at all, I'm just interested. You might make an awful lot of mistakes on the way. I meet people who have made too many mistakes and have never got anywhere. Had they gone the other way about it. . . .

RIGG How can you possibly have total companionship which is not based on a sexual knowledge of each other? You were talking about companionship afterwards.

McCULLOCH Well, you see, I think it is the other way round. One meets somebody and one goes gradually towards the physical expression. You are saying that you get the physical expression over first.

RIGG Because it is an obstacle.

McCULLOCH I just don't believe that. It may be an obstacle for you, but it wouldn't work like that for me. I think this is the most deep and intimate relationship there is, and you come to it very slowly. That is to say, you get to know the person in very many ways, first.

RIGG That would set sex, the sexual experience, as a pinnacle. I do not think of sexual experience as a pinnacle. I put the intellectual and the emotional experience as a pinnacle. Sex, after all, is a quite easy-to-attain commodity. To be utterly modernistic about it, it is presented everywhere: on hoardings, in advertisements, films;

this is a fact. Therefore what must be rich and rare after that is the personality, is the love, the soul, the spirit or whatever it is, of the person.

McCulloch I think you are right, absolutely right. I think the rich and rare thing is what you have described it—the mystery of two persons in relationship. But although there are rare people, like Abélard and Héloise, who could achieve complete sexual harmony the first time they ever saw each other, they *are* very rare and to put that down as the norm would be disastrous. Héloise and Abélard were very deep people already, and they met instantly and deeply, but most people only meet tangentially and casually, and to start off with sex at that point seems to me the most utter bathos and the most dangerous of activities. Sorry! I'm preaching at you.

Rigg Describe what you call the 'casual' surroundings?

McCulloch Well, if I meet a girl on a night out, or something, that would be casual. I would want to know her much, much more before I would get anywhere near intimacy of that kind.

Rigg Would you? How would you know that it wouldn't be another story of Abélard and Héloise?

McCulloch Well, I hope I would recognise it if it were! I hope your play will make people start arguing about this, because it seems to me the most valuable point of departure, so to speak, in the modern world. We've got to learn again, I think, how to know each other at depth and I don't believe you do it by diving in at the deep end first—you generally drown!

Rigg I don't think so—no.

12 May 1970

Unlike Dryden, I am expressing astonished admiration when I quote his lines to describe Jonathan Miller:

> A man so various that he seem'd to be
> Not one, but all mankind's epitome.

Jonathan, as I see him, is a kind of Renaissance figure; physician, actor, theatre director, satirist, literary critic, *et praeterea multum.* His tall frame surmounted apparently by the head of a friendly lion, would be best set off in late *quattrocento* costume. But if my wife is any criterion, the other sex takes very much to Jonathan's appearance just as he is, usually clad in pullover and slacks with a rough tweed coat which goes well enough with his dark auburn thatch.

In any age where good talk is a rare treat, Jonathan Miller would be justly rated as one of the most brilliant conversationalists of our time. He talks rapidly, vividly. The ideas and images in his mind pour forth on practically any subject, as though from the Pierian spring itself. He gestures impatiently when the channel of speech is for the moment too narrow to take the full flood of his thought. He has a rich treasury of words, almost Shakesperian in the bounty and imaginativeness of their use. I have never heard him utter a cliché except in jest.

For us, over the last few years, he has illuminated the dark days of early January by taking part in the opening dialogue of the new series, and at that time of the year his originality of mind and vigorous intellect are the sovereign antidote to the general Slough of Despond atmosphere in the City. Half an hour with Jonathan restores us, because clearly for him everything is perpetually a new prospect. His world is one of infinite possibilities and constantly new interest. The vision splendid never deserts him. He always leaves us feeling that it should and could be ours also.

DIALOGUE WITH

Jonathan Miller

McCulloch I wonder, Jonathan, if I might improve this far from shining January half-hour, by seeking your mind on a very well-worn, but still vexed problem: I mean that of the right relationship of male and female. Do you think equality is the most useful word in this context?

Miller The notion of equality for women seems to me to be self-evident, and almost something which is very hard to argue in favour of, simply because it is impossible to conceive of any arguments which could be held against it. Nevertheless, obviously, certain very acute practical problems are raised by this which are almost entirely concerned with the family, the way in which we rear our children and the sort of society which will arise as a result of altering these patterns. This is a very complicated problem and doesn't really have anything to do with the *equality* of women. It has something to do with the way in which men and women relate to each other and the way in which they, in turn, relate to the children which they produce.

McCulloch But apart from the children, isn't it true to say that there is a certain complementary balance between men and women, which exists whether they have children or not?

Miller Yes, I believe that the world is fundamentally *divided* by gender; that on the whole, our relationship to the world and our feeling about ourselves and about the world, is determined by gender. I don't think this is anything which can be obliterated except at great risk to the human personality. Men and women must always retain, I think, some complementary substance which jointly compiles the human substance and I cannot conceive of anything, short of a fundamental change in the biology of human beings, which will alter the fact that we are split down the middle in this way. Its outward signs are the fact that some people wear trousers and other people wear skirts, and that we excrete in different ways and so on, but there is, right at the core of our feeling, this split which can't be altered and which, in fact, gives us the feeling of being uniquely human.

McCULLOCH The curious thing is that people are awfully bothered by divisions in the human race at the moment—race relations and so on—and yet it seems to me that the most crucial thing in human life is this sense of maleness and femaleness, which appears to go so very deep into the human psyche.

MILLER This is something I feel very anxious about at the moment. I am rather opposed to the idea of resorting to biology in order to explain and justify certain standing relationships in human society. I think this is one of the most reactionary movements which is abroad at the moment—the idea that there are certain biological imperatives which determine human conduct, which cannot be overcome and which we disobey at our peril. The idea, for example, that human beings are fundamentally aggressive, that unless we understand this and acknowledge it, we cannot hope for success, which seems somehow to justify war, on the grounds that the survivor is the only successful man.

There is a whole series of reactionary doctrines which rest firmly on the idea that we are animals fundamentally, and that our human nature is something very fragile, based on biological foundations. Therefore I am very reluctant to make an exception with regard to the notion of gender and say that it is something which is biologically determined. I wonder what would be the case if some device could be introduced which could free females of conception and of pregnancy, whether in fact it would be possible suddenly to abolish this notion of gender.

McCULLOCH You are using the word 'gender' and I am using the word 'sex'. Is there a difference?

MILLER I use the word 'gender' simply because 'sex' has become so heavily polluted and——

McCULLOCH Overcharged, yes! I am interested in your last statement, because Bertrand Russell said that women in this age had been delivered from the twin fires of pregnancy and hell-fire. You know, religion had ceased to frighten them and they were no longer frightened of being pregnant.

MILLER Of course he is wrong there, because all they have been delivered from is the fear of unintentional pregnancy, but they haven't been delivered from the ordeal, or the trial, or the *pleasure* of pregnancy itself. The problem remains whether the distinction between the sexes would survive the complete removal of the biological process of pregnancy. Is it possible to conceive of a community where these distinctions were wiped out, do you think?

McCULLOCH I suppose it is possible that we might alter scientifically this particular biological aspect, but would we greatly affect thereby the way in which the masculine and feminine principles interact? I doubt it.

MILLER Well, shall we say that we would? But we are arguing simply, as it were, from the *status quo* of our society. Because a thing seems to be deeply rooted in our present experience, we assume that it is a fundamental imperative. There is a whole series of other developments which would have been rendered impossible if we were, in fact, rooted to our biological nature. It would seem unlikely, for instance, that we would build these sorts of buildings, and undertake the strange rituals that we do in them. It is a very curious thing, that reactionary policies almost always revert to biology and say, 'Well, that's the way it is, baby. Human nature is based on the flesh; man is an acquisitive, lecherous, family-making, territorial creature and there is no way of transcending this, and therefore let us have a capitalistic, aggressive, greedy, noisy society and treat with the biology within, and then we will have a peaceful society—based on war.' And it seems to me that this resort to biology is always the counsel of despair and denies the very thing which makes us human—our strange and unique capacity in the universe to *overcome* our biology.

McCULLOCH Quite. I agree! Now, do you subscribe to the theories of unisex, which so far, only the tailors have caught up with?

MILLER I'm not certain exactly what people mean when they talk about unisex. There are certain features in English society which stretch men and women apart and make them artificially distinct from each other. There is a certain idea that men are men, and their human identity is only realised when they are rugged, athletic, straightforwardly heterosexual, patriotic, acquisitive and family-defending. This seems to me as grotesque and distorting a doctrine as the idea that women are only women when they are domestic and child-bearing.

McCULLOCH And love putting plates in front of their men! Yes! Now, when these people carry banners and throw their underclothing into waste-paper baskets, what are they trying to say?

MILLER I think that it is very hard to know what people are saying when they make symbolic gestures. These often carry a whole series of messages which differ from person to person. They obviously are not what they seem to be on the surface. In many cases the tearing-off of brassières and putting them in dustbins is a symbolic act which represents women's image as having been imposed upon them by men who have tended in the past to regard them as decorative creatures, designed to provoke lust. It seems to me to be quite justifiable on women's part to reject this idea.

MCCULLOCH But what identity would they have if they could get it?

MILLER Well, it's not our place to ask that, in the sense that it is not our place to ask anyone, given freedom, what he would do with it. This is one of the things which is so appalling about the conservative doctrine—the idea that, 'Give these people money and they will put coal in their bath'. If that is what they want to do with their coal and their bath, it is not our business. The beauty of socialism is that it offers people the option to do what they like with their freedom, unless, of course, it interferes with, and violates the freedom of other people. It is a patronizing, paternalistic idea that, given freedom, certain people are ill-equipped to handle it and will exploit it.

MCCULLOCH But to go back to this word 'equality', it seems to me to be tied up with law. For most of mankind's history, women have had a rather subordinate position in human society, and presumably what they are now determined to have, is a full and equal position with the other sex. By all means let every citizen be equal before the law, but when you get down to what is, in fact, *personal,* equality becomes rather nonsense, doesn't it?

MILLER Not at all. It is there in fact that equality starts to have its meaning. The law itself is an extremely broad and provisional series of regulations which limit the extremes of human conduct, and permit certain transactions to take place. Where the *real* limitations of human freedom occur, is within those areas which law doesn't have anything to say about at all; things which determine whether people feel embarrassed or feel that they are violating social custom or habit. When women come to men, either aggressively or by entreaty, to ask for power or a change in their status, what they are asking for is nothing to do with the law at all. They are asking for a respect for their decisions on a par with those of men, and the law is silent on these issues.

McCulloch I agree. They feel that they have been confined for most of history in a subhuman status; that men have said that the realm of mind is their own and that women are truncated creatures who haven't really been equipped to think, and they must accept this. They are now refusing to accept it because they have had about a hundred years of what is called 'education' by males, and isn't this where the trouble starts?

Miller Well, I don't regard this as trouble, it's another moment in our joint development.

McCulloch But what males regard as education may be disastrous for women.

Miller It's disastrous for the current institution, as it stands. Of course, what women have to understand, when pressing for these various changes, is that equality and liberty are not just abstract principles but involve all sorts of fundamental changes in their status in the future. What happens about children? Do they still want to incubate children inside themselves for nine months, and nurse them, and be responsible in a unique way for their up-bringing? Or do they want, once the child has been voided, as it were, the process of raising to be undertaken, not just in *equality*, but in terms of absolute *identity* between the man and the woman? When you start altering the status of anyone you have to say, 'How are the institutions of society going to be different as a result of this particular series of changes in rights?'

McCulloch Way back in Genesis, it was stated that, 'God created man in his own image; male and female created he them'. I think that is one of the most remarkable statements of all time.

Miller Yes, it's a remarkable utterance, but I think it is a mistake to regard Genesis as 'way back', or as a comprehensive statement which embraces the whole of the human situation. This is a highly specialized statement about men and women which arises from a particular ethnic group, at a particular period in history, and it may well reflect the social institutions of the Jews at that particular period in history, *not* something about the human race as a whole.

McCulloch A thing must be estimated as true or false in its exact context. This was a statement, presumably, about the human race—that it can only find wholeness of personality by marrying maleness and femaleness in itself.

MILLER Yes, but nevertheless it's very hard to imagine what sort of social action could be based upon such a formula. It has a sort of resonant emptiness about it, that phrase. It seems to be true and yet one couldn't point to any consequence that could come of it. It seems convincing, as in certain sorts of ecstatic states of mind one is convinced, but one cannot actually be certain what one is convinced of.

MCCULLOCH Would you rub out all poetry, which is emotion?

MILLER No, but it's very hard to imagine how social policy is to be based on poetry.

MCCULLOCH Why not? But to get back to my problem—you either have to face now a possibility that you could rub out the whole question of sex in a few hundred years time, or the possibility that sex is ineradicable.

MILLER Well, I think it *is* ineradicable for several reasons. I don't believe that sex rests in the womb, nor is it the consequence of the womb. Here I am going against my own previous arguments in a sense, because I believe we inherit our sexual conduct because of the structure of our brain, or the structure of our pelvis. Our brain is at the service of our pelvis, it so happens, so that if the pelvis was altered so that our child-breeding was altered, we would still have the neurological apparatus of sexuality, and until one can alter that one is not going to be able to alter our notions of gender.

MCCULLOCH In other words, there are two kinds of humans—each approaching objective reality from opposite points of view?

MILLER I wouldn't necessarily think of it in such a right-hand-left-hand way. What I do believe is that we have, as a result of our neural organization, a tendency to approach each other, by and large, male towards female, in a way which has to do with lust. What I am saying is that sexuality is built into our brains and is taken up with negotiation between members of the opposite sex. It cannot be got rid of simply by altering the way in which we raise, breed and conceive our children.

MCCULLOCH Is sex so deeply embedded in human nature that the child business is really a by-product of it?

MILLER Well, I wouldn't say a by-product, because that seems to place it on a lower level. Child-rearing is part of this complex, but as I have said, the pelvis is not an *essential* part of sex.

McCULLOCH You agree then that sexual relations may result in children or they may not. Children are only incidental.

MILLER The fact that they are *now* incidental is a feature of our biochemical technology. Until we developed the Pill, this was not an optional relationship, now it is, and therefore we are brought face to face in a much more vivid way with the nature of the negotiation which takes place between men and women, as a thing in itself and not merely a precursor of breeding. But the relationship is controlled or *changed* by the fact that although you can separate sex and conception, conception depends upon sex. We still have to rear children and this seems to depend on men and women together, and on families. We have to work out how, in fact, we plan to raise our children and to reproduce the best features of the culture in the next generation which, after all, is what child-rearing is about.

McCULLOCH There is, then, in human nature, this division and you have to come to terms with what you are, male or female, and that if you are male you will, on the whole, approach life in a particular way.

MILLER I really don't feel that this is the case, entirely. This is an argument from the present state of society. We assume that to be male is identified with certain features we have already mentioned. This is an institutional, social feature of masculinity, it is nothing intrinsic to the gender itself. We have to register births—the sex of infants—in a Registry Office. What happens as a consequence of that act of registration seems to me to be very various indeed. I would be interested to see what happens in the course of the next fifty or a hundred years, to see how widely the options which go with one or other identity can be interpreted. I think, a great deal more widely than we feel at the moment. Which is why, for example, in certain levels of society, there is such infuriated maddened indignation when the problem of homosexuality comes up, because it terrifies people suddenly to see the clear-cut notions of one or other of these identities called into question. If you take away the guidelines which are associated with one or other gender, people are rather at sea.

McCULLOCH I am very interested, because you remember when Jesus visited the two sisters of Lazarus, Martha was busy getting the meal ready, and complained to Jesus that Mary was sitting at his feet, listening to him. And he must have upset everybody there by saying, 'Mary has taken the better part', in other words, 'She is doing the more important thing'. This must have been a revolutionary thing to say in a society where women were quite clearly supposed to be getting the meal instead of seeking for greater knowledge, which was what Mary was doing.

MILLER What I think is revolutionary is not so much turning the tables, but simply to open up the idea that there is no authorised role which goes with either one of the genders. This doesn't remove sexuality from the universe, it *does* mean that there are no specific roles or offices which go with one or the other necessarily. In this particular state of society there are these special roles but that is because society sets up its demands and then looks to biology to obtain what seem to be ineradicable credentials for its particular form of conduct.

McCULLOCH Peering into the future, do you think that the new civilization that we are hoping will come, will depend a great deal on the new way in which the sexes work out a better relationship, or not?

MILLER I think it is extremely important but I think it is a subsidiary part of a much larger problem—the way in which we handle personal identity and the notion of freedom in relation to other people. That is why there is already springing up this affinity between the Black Liberation movement and the Women's Liberation movement and the Students' Liberation movement. What we are on about now is the large problem of how we define our identities in a world which consists of a very large number—perhaps too many—of us. The problem is simply how we organize our institutions in such a way that we can each seem important.

12 January 1971